Tales from the
Playing Field

A new strategy for Business Management Coaching

Woodley & Watts

MONTREAL · SEDONA · TAOS

Tales from the
Playing Field

A new strategy for Business Management Coaching

Gilles R. Rochefort
B.Comm (SPAD), MBA

Woodley & Watts
400 McGill, 3rd Floor
Montreal, QC, Canada
H2Y 2G1

Canadian Cataloguing in Publication Data

Rochefort, Gilles R. (Gilles Rolland), 1952-
    Tales from the playing field : a new strategy for business management coaching

Includes index.
ISBN 0-9698972-7-8

    1. Supervision of employees. I. Title.

HF5385.R643 2000   658.3'02   C00-901446-2

Editor: Madeleine Partous
Editorial Coordinator: Sarah Rosenfeld
Cover design and graphics: Sylvie Arvanitakis
Text design: Grant Loewen

Printed in Canada

Acknowledgments

This book was made possible through the inspiration and involvement of many people over several years.

I thank Dr. Robert Wanzel and Greg Zorbas of Laurentian University for believing in my teaching abilities and allowing me the opportunity to do the coaching research.

Thanks to Dr. Ann Langley of Université du Québec à Montréal for the insight and analysis of the data that led to the theoretical model.

To James Day, wherever he is, thanks for the good coaching and the encouragement to persist with the project.

I thank the many managers, peers and subordinates I've had the privilege of working with in the last 25 years. Little do they know that each has had a hand in creating the story behind the model.

To Parkhurst Publishing, thanks to Madeleine Partous for believing in the project and making it a marvelous experience; and thanks to Sarah Rosenfeld for keeping the project on the rails.

Finally, thanks to my families – immediate, past, blended and extended – especially to my wife Cheryl and the children Rodrigue, Eric, Alex and Ryan. If the essence of life is human relationships, then I've been blessed with more than my fair share of truly loving ones.

Gilles R. Rochefort

Contents

Preface

Tales from the Playing Field is the result of 30 years of curiosity and frustration with the effects of good and bad coaching. My experience as an employee, manager, teacher, parent and coach, combined with a strong scientific argument for a new model, gave me the impetus to write this book.

The book is more than just a story about a middle manager trying to survive in a competitive environment. It's a lesson for all managers at every organizational level who are responsible for getting maximum performance out of their people, structures and processes. The coaching model presented in this book will be especially useful to business organizations that must understand and react quickly to the realities of today's volatile marketplace – whether they are in manufacturing, service or knowledge-based industries.

Tales from the Playing Field will appeal to first line supervisors and senior executives alike – it deals with performance and productivity issues that are found at all hierarchy levels and business functions in organizations today. People in Marketing, Sales, Operations, Finance, Information Technologies or Administration all stand to benefit from the unique approach of this powerful coaching model. The book also delves into personal issues that affect a manager's daily performance – from his or her relations at home to the relationships with peers, subordinates and superiors at work.

There are several reasons why I chose a novel to present the principles of effective business management coaching. First, I wanted the learning process to be entertaining as well as instructive. Second, I wanted people to see themselves in a character facing the same kind of pressures and opportunities they do – it makes the learning more meaningful. Third, the best way to demonstrate the effects of human relationships, both good and bad, are through fictional characters presented in a story that for some, may very well be true.

At the end of each chapter I've included some provocative questions and test questions to encourage the readers to do some introspection as well as evaluate their own coaching profile. In the last section of the book, tips and exercises are offered to help managers immediately affect their coaching effectiveness.

The development and testing of the coaching model followed the standard methodology for scientific experimentation – and the results supported the theory. The model, however, is new and the prescriptions are still being debated and improved. What the model needs most is more trials in other organizations around the world. Only then will the case of 'What is effective coaching?' be finally resolved.

Enjoy the story. Do the self-learning exercises. Try the model out for yourself. Be the best coach you can be.

Gilles R. Rochefort

Introduction

In the late 1950s, General Electric unveiled the results of an internal study in which 90% of the top managers credited a prior boss as the most important factor to their success.[*] From this study, the concept of "management coaching" emerged; so too did the debates surrounding the essence, the methods, the practices and the measures of "coaching."

Today, the term is used extensively in business as an essential attribute of an effective manager. Like in sports, competitive advantages in business can shift back and forth from period to period or quarter to quarter. Winning will depend on the ability of organizations to make swift and correct adjustments in their game plans to either defend their lead or make an offensive strike to acquire new market share. The responsibility for re-aligning the resources and executing the game plan rests largely on the shoulders of its managers, both staff and line. Their effectiveness in coaching their teams to make the required changes is proving to be a critical factor in determining the outcome of the game.

Still, the debate as to what constitutes effective coaching and how much it actually contributes to individual, group and organizational performance is far from over.

The story you are about to read can best be described as creative non-fiction. The story line is only partially true, but the coaching model is the result of empirical evidence I've gathered since 1993. The evidence reveals new insights into defining the essence and methods of coaching, as well as its empirical value to organizations seeking to acquire or sustain a competitive advantage in a changing marketplace.

[*] Lovin W.C. & Casstevells E.R., 1971.

Chapter 1

The Company

Preview _____

Meet James Treblid, the new Training Manager at MDL, a heavy
machine distributor in the Northeast. He's recently been hired to
find learning solutions in response to the escalating demand for
technical skills in the company's Sales and Service areas. But
there's something wrong with the fit between the company and
himself; the problem involves structures, processes, performance
and culture. If James is going to survive, let alone succeed, he
must find an answer very quickly.

It's 8:05 a.m. and -30°C outside. The car feels like an icebox and I feel like a dummy for sitting here. I'm mad at myself for not letting it warm up a bit before getting in. I can see my breath rolling up against the windows and sticking there like white paint. Until it warms up, it'll get worse. There's not much I can do except wait for the temperature to rise and melt away the layer of built-up frost.

I open my briefcase and pull out my cell phone, quickly punching in the numbers for my office. As I wait for the instructions to get into my voice mail, I flip open a note pad and get ready to write down messages.

"This is Lester Zaco. Meet me at my office this afternoon at 4. Click."

Whew! Not the kind of thing to brighten your day.

There are no other messages so I close the phone and put it away. I begin thinking about the day ahead. This is my third month at Machine Distribution Limited, or MDL, and I can't shake the lousy feeling I have about being there. And this phone call doesn't help.

At first I was excited when the V.P. of Human Resources at MDL called me for an interview for the Training Manager job; I couldn't help thinking it was going to be a great opportunity to validate a "coaching" model that I'd designed. Throughout the interviewing process, I talked about it with every manager I met. They liked it. So naturally, as the hiring process moved forward, my excitement at the prospect of finally testing the model also grew. But when the job offer came, I was disappointed; it didn't include a word about coaching. When I brought the matter up, I was told, "Yes, we recognize that coaching is a nice thing to have, but it's not a priority. There are more important and urgent matters that need your attention."

I was very disappointed.

I suppose I could have said no to the job, but I didn't. I convinced myself that hey, I could drive to work in 10 minutes and the pay wasn't bad. Besides, my model might still be useful.

But things didn't get better. I was new to the industry and my lack of knowledge showed. I knew little about the kind of management it took to run this kind of company and even less about the products it sold. I'd have to invest a great deal of time learning about everything – the products, technologies, customers and skills to be successful in this industry. It left little time to learn about the people in my department.

MDL's mission statement also scared me – "To service everything we sell within a day." Not an easy promise to keep at the best of times. The equipment was used for very punishing activities like mining, logging and other earth moving events. Sure it was designed for the work, but even with regular maintenance, the tremendous stresses put on the equipment virtually guaranteed that something was going to break at some point and a major repair would be needed. The competitive advantage went to the distributor who had the best product but especially the best product-support when the machines went down.

The new products were rife with high technology. Mechanics were learning to take out their laptops before their toolbox. The changes were rapid and spreading to all the product lines. The shift from mechanical to electronics was too rapid – the mechanics weren't keeping pace. MDL had over 9,000 machines in its territory. In the last eight years, it had doubled its product lines; in the last four, it had had to react to over 3,000 product modifications from the OEM. And given the kind of tortuous work the equipment was used for, the "24-hour service" commitment seemed more like a wish than a promise.

The day I truly understood my responsibility as the Training Manager was the day I realized how important the mechanics were to the business. These guys were the heart and brains of the Customer Service Division, and it was my job to make sure that they were trained on the right stuff and on time. They had to know products, technologies and processes inside out; they had to make the right diagnosis of machine problems with minimal down time. And to do it consistently meant continuous learning and, by extension, continuous training.

Keeping the sales force up-to-date on new products and product changes was also a challenge. The number of product launches and modifications were numerous and everyone seemed to be lagging behind.

The strange thing about all this was that the managers in both Sales and Customer Service didn't seem to plan their people's training in advance – as though they didn't know themselves what was coming down the manufacturer's production line.

≈

It's now 8:20. The windows are finally clear, so I back the car out of the driveway and start heading down the street. I can't go too fast. The roads are icy and school children are walking in the street. I catch a glimpse of my own boys, Max and Ty, and wave. They're difficult to miss. Max is fourteen and twice the size of any of his friends. His brother Ty is just the opposite. At ten he's barely half the size of Max. Walking side by side, they look like a wrestler and a jockey.

Max and Ty are my stepkids. Their mother Charlene and I have been married for eight wonderful years. I also have two children from a previous marriage, Derek and Sonja. They're in their twenties, working, and sharing an apartment downtown. We have what's called a "blended family." This is where everyone gets new relatives – parents, brothers, sisters, sons, daughters and of course in-laws. We all share the same core values, so the desire to be one big happy family is strong. We're lucky.

As the kids disappear from view, I pick up speed. I can't help thinking about the way things are going at work. MDL is a big company. It's part of a worldwide network of distributors. It purchases original manufactured equipment, sells it and backs it up with parts and service. The product line ranges from 240-ton trucks to hand-operated material handlers. The company is in its 52nd year of operations, has 1,100 employees and annual revenues of $400 million. It operates out of six Field Offices with its Corporate Headquarters and largest Customer Service Centre located in the Northeast.

I report to Roger Wicks, Director of Personnel. He in turn takes orders from Lester Zaco, Vice President, Human Resources, who also happens to be the one who first interviewed me. At the time, Zaco struck me as friendly and forthright. After being on the job for a few months, I learned otherwise. The relaxing eyes and fancy hairstyle would reveal a much more malignant personality.

Zaco and three other Vice Presidents – Finance, Sales, and Customer Service – report to the CEO, Hugh Cones. Together they form the Executive Committee and establish policy and strategy for the organization. Some people jokingly call it the King's Club.

MDL also has six General Managers – they report to both the Vice President of Sales and the Vice President of Customer Service. The GMs manage the Field Offices and have the dual responsibility for both sales and customer service in their territory. The two VPs and six GMs meet regularly to discuss plans and performances. This group is called the Management Committee and is accountable to the Executive Committee. Typically, they set the objectives for each Field Office and communicate the ways and means to achieve them.

Given that all strategic and tactical decisions are made between these two groups, there is very little decision-making left for the 60 middle managers that report to them. And this includes staff managers like my boss, Roger and of course, me.

The company was far from being a big happy family. It's not what I expected. Power and politics seemed to take precedence over productivity and teamwork. In spite of a common drive for profits, the company was clearly divided by the lines drawn between the two main business groups, Sales and Customer Service. The first was responsible for selling the machines and the Customer Service or CS group was responsible for fixing them when they broke down – within 24 hours of course!

It was easy to understand why these two groups fought so much. I'd often heard the Sales VP say, "We're in the business of selling heavy machinery, and so it's the job of Sales to set the pace and direction for the organization." He might have added, "Like it or not." Oddly enough, the CS people and those of us in the Corporate group usually agreed with them. But sometimes we didn't. And it occasionally got pretty nasty. The CS guys got fed up with the patronizing attitude of the Sales group. They contended that many of the customer beefs stemmed from the moment the machine was sold. They'd say, "Sales reps should take some responsibility for the complaints, cut down on their arrogance and fix the situation." The Customer Service VP concurred. "The Sales reps aren't motivated to stick around. They're paid on commission and so once a deal is done, they're off to find their next sale."

The Sales group, however, saw the problem differently. They felt that customer complaints were the result of poor after-sales support. They claimed that the CS group didn't meet the service standards and were solely responsible for clients complaining about late deliveries and slow repairs.

A lot of energy was spent on finding fault and little on accepting responsibility and solving the problem. Stories of preparing business cases and convening meetings to confront each other were legendary.

Roger Wicks, my boss, hadn't been much help either. From the start, I sensed his concern about his own job. He pretended not to be bothered by the fact that Zaco, his boss, called me personally for an interview. I later learned that Zaco leaned pretty hard on him to hire me. Knowing Zaco, I could see him smiling and saying to Roger "…it's your responsibility, but this is what I strongly urge you to do…" So I'm skeptical when Roger scratches his graying head and tells me, "It's no big deal." Right.

When I consider all this, it's hard to be in Training and feel good about it.

17

I'm on the highway now. Traffic is heavy, but it doesn't matter because I take the first exit anyway. Even with traffic, the whole exercise is relatively stress-free. Just the thought of not having to fight my way into the city morning and night relaxes me. Getting to work is actually relaxing. It's a good time to reflect on things. The driving becomes unconscious and so my thoughts turn to the Training Department

The history of the Training department is somewhat checkered. Twenty years ago, trainers worked in an environment where the variety of products was limited and the computer technology was still undeveloped. The CS Vice President managed the department. Ten years later, with a downturn in the economy, Training department resources were slashed. Apprenticeship programs for mechanics were canceled, trainers were moved to other areas of the organization and systematically all training activities were pared down or eliminated. It remained that way for several years.

In spite of improved market conditions, the 90s didn't start out as a happy period for the department either. More trainers were hired and the department was transferred from the CS group to HR in the Corporate group. Trainers, all mechanics themselves, didn't like it. Reporting to someone in Personnel, as they called it, was a blow to their self-esteem. To make matters worse, the first thing Zaco did was to centralize decision-making and take direct control of every aspect of training from his office at Corporate Headquarters. This didn't enhance his image with the training department nor the training department's reputation – especially in the field offices where "Personnel" were viewed more or less as paper-pushing policemen.

The last few years have been tough on the Personnel Managers too. Roger is now the fourth manager in six years. Resignation, burnout and dismissals are given as the reasons for the high turnover. Roger has an incredibly heavy workload. Over and above his duties in personnel administration, his mandate includes planning and implementing all corporate and technical training programs for internal employees as well as providing training to many of the customers that buy our machines. The Training department sells its services to outside customers – those that buy our machines and prefer to fix them themselves. Roger's job is to maximize these revenues. This alone is a contentious issue between the Sales and CS groups. The Sales reps like it because it gives them another feature to sell with the machines. The CS reps hate it because it reduces the potential for service and parts sales – and their commissions. So if Roger succeeds in making "Training" a profitable or at least a break-even operation, it's a bonus for the department, but maybe not for the company – especially given that parts and service revenues offer the biggest profit margins by far. This situation doesn't promote harmonious relations between Training and the Sales and CS groups. And given the limited resources of the department and the fact that Roger's performance appraisal is largely based on how well the Sales and CS groups like him, it's not surprising he's a nervous wreck.

All in all, Roger has a very difficult job. And his personal insecurity doesn't help make the situation any easier for him or the people reporting to him.

〜〜

It's 8:30 and I turn into the parking lot. Because the Head Office houses the largest Customer Service Centre, the parking lot is usually full. The 200 or so mechanics arrive at 7:00 and the office staff between 7:30 and 8:30. I'm always among the last ones to arrive. And so, once again, I park at the far end of the lot and prepare for the chilly five-minute walk from my car to the front door of the building. At least this morning I'm well dressed for it. I wrap a scarf around my neck, put on my gloves and step into the deep freeze. Hmm! The cold isn't that bad. As I make my way towards the main gate, I keep thinking about the difficulties of the day ahead.

My position is a newly created one. As the Training Manager, I support Roger in achieving departmental goals and manage the Training department. The department now has 10 trainers and a secretary. My role is to define training needs, assign trainers and make sure participants transfer their newfound knowledge and skills back to the job.

Before starting at MDL, Zaco made it clear to everyone that in this newly created position my contribution would be one of management and instructional design, not technical or product-related. I was expected to manage resources with a view to keep Sales, Customer Service, Corporate and outside customers happy. This seemed appropriate in light of my background.

But the reality is different. Because I don't have a strong background in the industry, products, processes or technologies, I'm really disadvantaged. It would take me at least two years, if not more, to get a respectable working knowledge of some of these things. The technology involved in servicing the machines alone is very complex and would never come naturally to me. I'm not a mechanic and wasn't going to become one any time soon! To pretend otherwise would be unrealistic and stupid.

I really have to wonder who is crazier, the company for offering me the job or me for taking it.

♒

I finally arrive at the security gate. I show my pass to the guard and enter the building.

There are three pedestrian entrances into the building. Uniform guards control two of the entrances, but the third only requires a passkey. The main entrance is for visitors only and they're required by the receptionist to sign in and carry a Visitor's pass. Then there's the entrance for middle managers, hourly employees and office staff. Here, everyone must show identification on the way in. On the way out, any item too big for a lunch pail to conceal requires a written authorization by any middle manager, no less. Items include books, writing pads and tools of course. Laptop computers and software programs don't need written authorization. Go figure. Finally, there's the private entrance for Senior Managers. They have a key. I find the inconsistency in the system more degrading than annoying. It suggests control, mistrust and paranoia. I don't like it.

Past the security gates are the Administration Offices. Here the entire Corporate group is located on one floor. The President, Vice Presidents, and several General Managers are here. We call it the "Bunker." The walls are colourless, windows are non-existent and every office door is shut. In the centre of the bunker is a pool of secretaries who are glued to their computer screens or running from office to office. Rarely is anyone caught having a casual conversation in this area.

Roger's office is here too, next to Zaco's.

My office, on the other hand, isn't here. It's at the other end of the plant, a good 10-minute walk from the security gate and the Bunker.

As I walk through the plant, I'm reminded of how non-technical I am. I might know some of the names of the different shops, and a little on what they do, but I don't have a clue as to why or how. The sound of impact drills and the smell of hot metal fill the air. I see "MACHINING," "ENGINE REBUILDS," "HYDRAULICS" and am totally mystified by it all.

I walk through a set of doors at the end of the shops and turn left. I follow a long corridor and turn right at "THE CAFETERIA." In a few minutes I pass the hustle and bustle of the "PARTS DEPARTMENT" and of "SHIPPING & RECEIVING." It's a beehive – phones ringing, paper shuffling and people moving about. I head up two flights of stairs to the second floor. At

20

the top is the "TRAINING DEPARTMENT." I open the door and walk in, all in a sweat. The air is cool. Soft music can be heard in the background over the distant squeals of impact drills. There's no sunlight here either, but the walls are lined with shelves stuffed with books, binders and videotapes. Schematics, prints, charts, calendars, anything colourful are plastered over the rest.

I used to wonder if my being so far away from the Bunker was by design or default. I quickly discovered that being out of sight was more than symbolic. The Training department's input into business strategies wasn't sought or acknowledged. Being at the other end of the building is exactly where we're meant to be. Pity.

〜〜

Rose, my secretary, is the first to greet me. "Good morning, Mr. Treblid," she says in her warm, formal manner. I hate it when she calls me "Mister." I must've told her a hundred times to call me James, but she won't. Rose is in her early 50s and has been with the company for 30 years. She was obviously trained to call her bosses "Mister." I have a good relationship with Rose and understand it's done out of respect. But I don't want her to think I agree.

"Good morning, Rose," I say, shaking my head with the usual "I wish you wouldn't" look. But then I smile. I go past her desk and walk into my office. The lights are already turned on, so I take off my winter boots and hang up my coat. As I turn towards my desk, Rose is standing in the doorway and says, "Mr. Treblid, Mr. Wicks called and would like to see you this afternoon at two."

I think to myself, I know why too! Roger's concerned about the complaints from the mechanics. I tell Rose to call him and confirm that I'll meet him at 2 p.m. I don't sit down, but head instead towards the coffee machine. Without paying attention to what's happening around me, I pour myself a cup and head right back to my office. This time I close the door and continue with my thoughts.

The odd thing about my office is that it's an inner corner office with two very large windows. Rose's desk is directly in front of my door, so when it's closed I can't see her, but there are days when I feel like I'm in a fishbowl. When people are milling outside my office, anyone can see in. I can't scratch myself without checking first to see if anyone's watching. Closing the door keeps the noise out, but not much else.

I stare into space. I still feel lousy. I realize that as the weeks go by, I'm becoming very cynical about the whole thing, finding it more difficult to adapt to the culture of MDL. I find Roger harder to work with; his direction is fuzzy and for some reason he's becoming more and more inaccessible.

It's clear to me that if I'm going to stick it out with this company, I've got to do something different. I've got to get to the decision-makers, find a way to get my coaching model on the corporate agenda.

Obviously, I need a plan to get there!

What About You?

- Is your industry technology driven?

  _____

  _____

  _____

- How would you describe the culture in your company?

  _____

  _____

  _____

- How would you describe the politics within your company?

  _____

  _____

  _____

- How dependent is your job on getting 'real time' information?

  _____

  _____

  _____

TEST YOURSELF and your SUPERVISOR _____

Answer each statement according to the following scale:
Almost never - 1   Sometimes - 2   Regularly - 3   Almost always - 4

1. In your work group (department),
   people are encouraged to take
   initiatives to solve problems.   1   2   3   4

2. In your work group, people get the
   chance to utilize their skills.   1   2   3   4

3. In your work group, people trust
   each other.   1   2   3   4

4. In your work group, people have a
   feeling of self-accomplishment.   1   2   3   4

5. From your perspective, your internal
   and external customers like working
   with your work group.   1   2   3   4

6. Your work group solves customer
   problems.   1   2   3   4

Chapter 2

The Situation

Preview _____

James comes face to face with the problems that are affecting the
organization, his department and himself as a manager. Through a
series of animated and sometimes humorous encounters, he is
confronted with issues of productivity, credibility and control.
He'll also meet "the boss" and discover that he's not to be trusted.

I look at my watch. Jeez! It's almost 9:00 o'clock! Where's my agenda? Okay, here it is. First I meet George Pike, the Customer Service Manager for this Field Office at 9:30; then Frank and Larry, two of my trainers, at 11:00; and Roger at 2:00. And let's not forget his boss, Zaco, at 4:00.

I hope Roger will be there this time. The last time there were just the two of us and I found out later that Roger was hovering around Zaco's office wondering what we were talking about. Of course he never asked me directly. I wonder what this meeting is going to be about. The last time Zaco wanted my views on the optimum ratio of instructor to participants in the classroom. He then proceeded to lecture me on the importance of training efficiencies. What he meant of course was cramming as many people as possible in each class. I don't have a problem with maximizing efficiencies, but I do if it's at the expense of learning. Anyway, I hate it when Zaco meets with me alone. It's gamy and does nothing to boost Roger's confidence.

I push it out of my mind for now. First things first. George Pike will be here in a few minutes.

I've heard that he's been complaining to Roger about the training department for some time. He says he doesn't understand what we're doing, and would like to see an easier system for scheduling. He would also like shorter training classes – like half days at a time. He feels that two- and three-day classes are too long. His operations can't manage it.

Generally, I think I like George. I met him on two other occasions with Roger. He's a gregarious type – over six feet with a booming voice. But he's best known for his direct approach and southern accent – customers like him for it. He earned his position as Service Manager by coming up through the ranks; he started as an Apprentice Mechanic and moved all the way up to Field Mechanic. After spending five years as a Shop Foreman, he was promoted to Service Manager three years ago. He's been with the company for 15 years so he knows the ropes.

George is political, smart and emotional. He's dedicated to customer service and obsessive about profit margins. I find it strange, though, that he complains about the lack of training his people receive on the one hand and in the same breath feels compelled to justify why he pulls his people out of training classes because of rush jobs in the shops. In the past, he's proposed to have training at night, after the mechanics have finished their regular shifts. This would ensure, as he puts it, "that we stop pissing away money because people are in school." I think he wants to meet with me to go over this again.

I scurry to prepare. From the corner of my eye I see George arriving.

My office door flies open – and there's George. "Good morning, Jimmy." He extends his big hand and I get up to shake it.

"Hi, George, come in." I try my best to sound just as enthusiastic.

"Jimmy," he says in a no-nonsense tone, "I know you're the new kid on the block, so let's you and me have a talk sort of 'mano a mano.' If ya know what I mean."

Trying to use my best Texan accent, I say, "Sure! What's on your mind pardner?"

He laughs and says, "You know, Jimmy, I've talked about this in the past with Roger, but now we really have to do something. I figure if I talk directly into the horse's mouth we might be able to reach some sort of mutual understanding about your training schedule. D'ya understand what I'm saying?"

"I get it George. Go on."

"Well, how can I expect to run a shop if my foremen are always complaining that their people are spending half their time sittin' on their asses in class? Everything is moving faster 'round here. Customers don't want to wait – Hell, they can't afford to wait! Every hour their machine is down, they're losing money. And that's not all. My boss is squeezing like a boa constrictor for more margins. There're rumours about cutting people. Can you imagine that? I think they're trying to tell us something. What do you think?"

And before I can get a word in, George keeps on going. "My guess is, it's early in the year and we'd better get our asses in gear or they'll start mopping bodies off the shop floors and maybe in some of these offices too. I don't mean to scare ya, but we've got to make some changes. You're a lucky fella, Jimmy, 'cause all you have to worry about is scheduling training classes."

I suddenly feel hot but decide to ignore the feeling and say nothing about the comment.

George goes on, "Anyhow, that's why I'm sittin' here. We need to find a better handle for getting our technicians up to speed on the new machines. My foremen don't know how and don't have the time. It's your job, why should they do it? The problem is that you guys are holding us up – your training is either late or in the way, take your pick. I've got profits to make, but every time we get a new machine my boys don't get trained on 'em or you've got 'em in class just when we need them in the shops the most. By the way, we call them 'technicians' now – as if it makes a big difference to the guy who's paying! Anyhow, do you understand what I'm saying here, Jimmy?"

I nod without giving the slightest hint of the rising temperature inside my shirt collar. I don't mind being called "Jimmy." It's the attitude that's getting me hot.

"Am I going too fast here?"

I shake my head and can barely get a "no" out.

George continues, "What I'm driving at here is that we need some wholesale changes in the way you guys are running the training schedule. Far be it for me to start telling you how to do your job, but dammit, Jimmy, I'm losing $100 per hour for every technician who's in training during the day shift! Did you know that?"

"No," I reply icily.

His voice is rising to a new pitch. "Sure," he says, pointing both fingers at me like they were six-guns. "Look, with wages and benefits, a gall-darn technician costs me $25 per hour from the time he punches in to the time he punches out – whether he's twiddling his thumbs or actually working. Now if he's repairing a customer machine, I don't mind paying it, because the customer is paying me 75 bucks per hour in labour plus any parts we put in. That's $50 in gross profit on the labour alone! Now – and stay with me on this because this is the important part – if the mechanic, I mean the technician, is in training, it's not only costing me $25 an hour for the guy's wages but it's also costing me at least $75 in lost revenues. And that, my friend, is $100 per hour in opportunity cost! And I just can't afford it. Do you see what I mean, buddy?"

I'm getting very hot now, but I don't want to get into a fight with George this morning – I'm not ready. Still, I don't want to leave him with the impression that I don't understand or care about his problems either. And most of all, I don't want him to think that I agree with his line of thinking on the "$100 opportunity cost" thing. So I begin my response by shaking my head like I just heard the saddest story of my life. And with as much compassion as I can muster I say, "George, you've got big shoes to fill. And if I were in them, I'd probably feel the same way you do. You're expected to make money, keep your customers happy and make sure your people are trained. It's like a baseball manager telling his pitcher, who's in a jam, 'throw strikes but don't give the batter anything good to hit.' It's an almost impossible situation. Right?"

"You bet!" George says.

"Look, as you've said, I'm new here – so it's hard for me to fully appreciate the pressure you're under. So I won't tell you that I understand exactly how you feel, because I don't."

He nods approvingly.

"But let me tell you where I'm coming from. This whole matter is more complex than just shifting training from daytime to nighttime. From my point of view, if you want your guys to keep fixing these machines in a reasonable time frame and still make some money, then we need to find a way to continually upgrade their knowledge and skills so that they meet your customer needs. This means getting your foremen involved and getting your technicians to learn on their own. And we have to leverage training resources too – I'm accountable for it. Finally, we gotta do all these things without burning out everybody in the process – and that means your technicians and my trainers. Do you understand what I mean?"

"Yup," he says flatly.

I continue, "With the rates we charge now, our customers have a tough time as it is paying for mechanics standing around trying to figure out a problem with their machines, let alone paying them for finding out how it works in the first place."

He doesn't react.

I go on. "To say nothing of the complexity that has grown with each new generation of products we sell. Why do you think we're changing our mechanics' names to "technician"? It's because the new name suits them – grease monkeys with computers. I did a little survey recently. And do you know what I found out?"

No reaction from George.

"I asked one question to 25 of our technicians who had taken a specific training class in the last six months. The question was made up by the trainer and was basic to the course. Do you know that only three guys got the right answer? Three out of 25! When I asked them what happened, they said, "We never get to practice on the new machines." So, George, how do you expect them to be motivated, let alone remember what they've learned? Everything is moving fast for everyone. By moving training around so as not to interfere with the day-to-day operations is not the only answer. Your foremen have to make sure that your technicians get a chance to practice what they learn in class, you know, on-the-job kind of training."

George grimaces.

I try to put on the brakes, but I can't. "And another thing you said, 'about losing money because of opportunity cost' – don't you think that your guys make you a lot more money in the long run by knowing how to fix the machines right the first time? That's what keeps your customers happy – 'every job done within 24 hours,' remember? The next time you calculate your opportunity cost you should recognize the value of the knowledge and skills your technicians learn during the time they're in training. Factor it into your formula and you might find that it's making you money!"

I can tell by the flush in George's face that he's getting impatient and annoyed. He's silent. I recognize the look of contempt on his face. I should, because I've had it on my own face a few times when dealing with people in the Personnel department. It's the kind of look that says, "You just don't get it, do you?"

I finally calm down and take a deep breath. I wanted to avoid an argument with George this morning, but that's exactly where we've landed. I'd better back off for now. I decide to take a conciliatory tone and say, "George, I want to think about this a little bit – especially the bottleneck we seem to be creating for you – and get back to you. But in the meantime, how about if we schedule some training in both the afternoon and evening for now and see how it goes? We'll split the training between daytime hours and evenings. This way, you have your people in the shops in the morning. In the afternoon, they would attend classes. And if necessary, we'll schedule only evening classes so we don't screw up your daily operations."

George's eyes light up and jubilantly responds, "Now you're talking, Jimmy Boy! I knew all along that if I explained the seriousness of the situation, you'd understand. You're pretty smart – I like that." Before I can say anything more, he springs to his feet, gives me a "thumbs-up" and with a big grin walks out of the office.

I hear myself saying – George Pike, you son of a bitch. You got exactly what you wanted but didn't care to understand my point of view. When it comes to training, that's exactly the attitude I keep seeing – if I agree with the Sales and CS groups, I'm smart; if I don't, it's because I don't get the real business issues. I shake my head.

I know this much. If our company is depending on technology to maintain a competitive edge in the marketplace, it had better find a way to accommodate the learning for it too. Our technicians want it and the company needs it. And besides, I'm sick and tired of being seen as the "bottleneck" in the system. This needs to be rectified.

I finally calm down.

I write down some notes about the meeting and pull out two bright-yellow file folders and write "BOTTLENECKS" on one of the tabs and "DESIRE/SLACK" on the other. I place the files on the corner of my desk.

〰

After finally shaking the emotions of the first meeting I begin to think about the next one with Frank Vienna and Larry Yates, a couple of trainers.

I've got 20 minutes before they arrive. I get up and get a fresh cup of coffee, wondering why they want to meet with me, but I suspect they're not happy with the workload they have. I've been loading them up with a lot of training assignments lately. And when they hear about doing evening classes, well! As it is, I've been hearing rumblings about too little time to prepare their classes and too much out-of-town travel; between going to the manufacturer for weeks at a time for new product training and the constant pressure to develop new training programs, they're getting tired. I can see it. No one's talked to me directly about their gripes and maybe the meeting is about something else after all. It seems wise to keep an open mind and see what they have to say.

I watch them arrive and get up to greet them. They sit down like there were needles sticking out of the seat.

When I met Frank for the first time, his great head of silver hair is what struck me most. As a former mechanic with 20 years at MDL, he's earned the respect of his peers in the department and the managers and technicians in the shops. He's low-key, hardworking and always gets the job done with no fanfare.

Larry, on the other hand, has virtually no hair at all. In spite of being with the department only a few years, he's easily the most sociable trainer of the bunch – he'll talk to anybody. But he's also very opinionated – says what's on his mind, like it or not. He and I have never had a run-in, but I know Roger has, on more than one occasion. What I like about him is that he doesn't appear to hold any grudges – he blows up and it's over.

Both trainers have reported to several new bosses in the last few years. Roger is the last of a series of Personnel Directors. And now there's me. The scuttlebutt is that Training Managers are as expendable as Personnel Directors are. So my feeling is that they don't see me as long-term either.

"Hi, Frank, Larry. Come in, please."

I sense their discomfort, so I try to put them at ease. "I heard a funny joke the other day. There's this Training Manager walking in the park with two of his trainers during their lunch break. They come across this magic lantern. The Manager picks it up and rubs it. Suddenly a Genie appears, and says, "It's your lucky day, lads; you each get a wish. So what'll it be?" The first trainer says, "I want to be on an island in the South Pacific, surrounded by servants and beautiful women." The Genie laughs and replies, "No problem, here's your wish." And suddenly the trainer disappears! The second trainer ponders for a moment and says, "I wish I was King of a Medieval Castle with an army at my disposal." Poof! He's gone too. The Genie turns to the Training Manager. "And what about you?" Without missing a beat the guy replies: "I wish that my two trainers are back at their jobs right after lunch!"

They both explode with laughter. I think they like the joke. Or maybe they're just nervous.

Larry grins. "The moral of that story is that you should never make a wish before your boss does!" They laugh again.

The ice is broken.

"You guys called the meeting. What's on your mind?"

Frank starts nervously. "James, you seem like an okay guy, so don't take this personally."

Right away I'm thinking this isn't a good way to begin. It's hard not to expect the worse.

"I'll try not to," I say as engagingly as I can.

Before Frank can continue, Larry takes over. "James, we're on the verge of mutiny here! The department is totally disorganized! There's no leadership and we're all fed up!"

There's silence.

Frank nudges Larry and goes on more calmly. "James, we're not blaming you for the situation. You've only been here a few months. These problems were around long before you arrived. But at the same time, we don't see how someone with virtually no experience in our business, let alone our company, can turn things around."

Again, silence.

I clear my throat. "What you're saying is that because the department is rudderless and because I'm new here and don't have any real experience in this industry, I can't do much to improve the situation. Is that it?"

Frank says, "That's part of it."

"What else?" I say calmly.

"We're asked to train on things we don't even know ourselves yet. New machines show up in the yard and no one knows about them. Suddenly the sales guys are down our backs for information and the CS guys are in a panic because they need to service them and don't know how. How are we supposed to help them if we haven't been trained on them ourselves? This is what Larry means by disorganization and lack of leadership. We'd all like to know where we're going so we can be ready when these new machines show up."

"I see your point, Frank. If sales reps and mechanics are waiting for training, then we're bottlenecks in the system. And we all know what happens in a bottleneck. Pressure mounts and people look for blame. And we're an easy target for the Sales and CS guys."

They nod, relieved.

"Does everyone here feel the same way?"

They nod again.

Showing no emotion, I say, "Okay. I respect your opinions and think I get the point. Listen, I'm meeting Roger this afternoon and I'd like to bring this up with him." I pause. "Let's schedule a meeting for the day after tomorrow with all the trainers. We'll go over all the issues and take it from there." Again I pause. "Look, I can't promise anything now. All I ask for is that you give me a chance and a couple of days to get back to you."

Frank nods and gently says, "James, I'm sure you can appreciate that this isn't the first time we've raised these matters with our bosses before."

Larry grumbles, "And there's been a bunch of 'em."

Once again, like the voice of reason, Frank nudges Larry and then looks up at me. "James, try your best. We'll see you in a couple of days."

They walk out. As they pass by Rose, she turns to me. I can see the concerned look on her face. I'm thinking to myself, here are a bunch of people who are trying to do their jobs as best they can, but they feel lost, running blind, forced to accept blame for things they don't control, and on top of that they've got no confidence in their boss.

〰

What a morning. I felt bad already when the day began and now I'm beginning to get scared.

I look at my watch and it's only 11:30, but I'm starving. I'll grab a quick sandwich and get ready for my meeting with Roger.

As I walk out of the training area and head down the stairs towards the cafeteria, I hear "James! Wait up!"

I turn. It's Charles Renacks, the Group Sales Manager. He's dressed like he should be working at a bank, not a Heavy Machine Distributor – navy blue suit, button-down shirt and a Rolex.

In a surprisingly squeaky voice he says, "Can I join you for lunch? "

"Sure." Really all I wanted was a damn sandwich and time to stew at my desk.

"You know, James, we're off to one of the best starts ever. Our reps are going gangbusters. And you deserve a lot of credit!"

"Oh?"

"Oh, yes. Listen, offering customer training at the end of a deal as an added value feature is a real strong closing point. Clients love it. And they really love your trainers. They're professional and really know their stuff."

"Thanks! I'm sure they'll be happy to hear it too. I'll pass it along."

We enter the cafeteria and Charles grabs my arm from the side and says, "There's one thing, though, I'd like to discuss with you. Do you mind if we do it now?"

"Go ahead." I tell him.

"No, no. Let's get our food first."

We each pick up a food tray and line up for the luncheon special – soup and sandwich. As we approach the cash, Renacks says "It's on me."

"Thanks, Charles."

We sit in a quiet corner of the cafeteria and Charles starts the conversation where he left off.

"James, my sales reps love offering our customers 'training' as part of a deal. And I'm certain you know that the demand for it is growing too. But I have a problem. The guys are complaining that a lot of the training is being scheduled several months after the machine has been sold and delivered. Is that true?"

"Sadly, yes, in some cases it is." Charles pulls out a pen and a pad from his shirt pocket and starts to take notes. I continue. "Because the technology is changing at such a frantic rate, our own technicians are having trouble keeping up – and we've made them our priority. Do you know that, in the last year, we've doubled the amount of in-class training for them? The result is that customer training is being pushed back. Our trainers are overloaded and can't satisfy everyone's needs as quickly as we would all like.

There's also the confusion surrounding the direction we're given by management. As you probably know, our senior managers are divided about whether we should even be doing customer training in the first place. The CS managers strongly believe we're shooting ourselves in the foot by showing our customers how to service their own machines. 'Service,' they say, 'is our biggest margin maker.' The Sales group, on the other hand, argues that it's strategic to have our customers know our machines better. They claim that in the long run, customers will buy more machines and more parts. Besides, as they like to say, 'We don't have to show the customers everything!' What this means is that we're being pulled in two different directions. And so we had to make a decision to defer some of the customer training until someone gives us a clearer direction as to who should get it and how much of it they should get."

Charles takes more notes and says, "You've made some very good points. I can see your challenge in trying to balance everyone's needs. It's not an easy situation for anyone." He continues to write.

I'm impressed with Charles. Other than the fact that he has two Regional Sales Managers reporting to him, I don't know much about him. But he takes notes and shows some empathy for our situation. It's actually quite refreshing.

He closes his pad and says, "Let me go back to my people and see if we can't work something out. I'll call you back to tell you the outcome."

"Great!"

Without another word, he picks up his tray and walks away.

I feel pretty good about the conversation and turn around to take another look at Charles' retreating back. To my surprise he stops and sits down at another table. I focus on the person who's already sitting there. It's Lester Zaco. My warm, fuzzy feelings evaporate.

〰〰

I walk out of the cafeteria, a little perplexed by what I just witnessed.

"Jim!" The voice is familiar. I turn and it's my friend Mike, one of the few people I knew before coming here.

"Hi, I saw you were having lunch with Charles," he says.

"Yeah." Now I've got mixed feelings about the whole thing. Looking for some insight, I turn to Mike. "You worked for him at one time, didn't you?"

"Yeah, three years ago when he was a Regional Sales Manager."

"He seems to take a real interest in people. What's he like?"

With a definite edge, Mike responds, "He's an asshole, buddy."

"Excuse me?" I ask, surprised.

Mike measures his words and tone carefully. "I wouldn't trust the son of a bitch for anything." Then he pauses. "I used to think Charles was okay as a boss. He seemed to take a real interest in his people's development, both professionally and personally. If you had a personal problem, you could go to Charles and always find a sympathetic ear."

"So what happened?"

"One day, I'm in the locker room at the gym, toweling down after a work-out. I hear voices from the other row of lockers and recognize Charles's. As I tune into their conversation, I can't believe what he's saying. He's joking with another MDL manager about very personal matters he and I talked about. I was furious. That afternoon, I went to his office and confronted him with it. He denied everything. I was so mad, I immediately asked for a transfer. And got it. I now report to Dan Wetomy. He's not as refined as Charles is, but as a Regional Sales Manager he's earned the respect of his reps through example. I like him." Mike pauses for a moment, then adds, "It's too bad that ever since Charles was promoted to Group Sales Manager, Dan has to report to him." He gazes at me intently. "Jim. Just watch out."

"Thanks. I will."

∿

I finally make it back to my office, a little unsettled by Mike's story.

The phone rings and it's Roger, my boss. "James, gotta cancel our meeting this afternoon. Something's come up. Can we do it next week, say Thursday?"

I get a little aggressive. "Roger, wait a minute! We've got to talk. I had a meeting with Frank and Larry this morning. Everyone up here is very upset with the way things are going. It can't wait; you and I have to discuss this today!"

"Yes, I know all about it, James. A couple of the guys came to see me this morning around 11:00."

I can't hide my impatience. "So what did you say?"

"Basically, I said we'd look into it."

"That's it?"

"There's nothing I can do about this right now. Anyway, it's your job. Take care of it."

I can't believe it. "But Roger, I told them we'd meet them on Friday

36

and go over the situation. If we wait until next week, it'll destroy whatever credibility I have. And the lid on this thing could blow at any moment!"

"Look, if it makes you feel any better, send me your agenda by e-mail and I'll see if I can squeeze you in somewhere this Thursday. Okay?" And before I can reply, he says, "Listen, gotta run," and hangs up.

The day is suddenly taking a turn for the worse.

I lean back in my chair and hear myself saying aloud, "Treblid, you're in deep shit now." The department's going to Hell and my idiot boss is probably going ice fishing! Great!

I wonder how hard it would be to find another job?

〰

It's 3:45. Zaco wants to meet me at 4:00, so I'd better get going.

After a brisk walk through the shops I arrive in the Bunker. Zaco's secretary sees me and waves me to wait in the reception area just off his office.

Lester Zaco is a strange guy. We arrive to work at about the same time in the mornings and when I run into him he barely acknowledges me. He spends most of his day with his office door closed and the only way his employees can talk to him is by scheduling an appointment several days ahead of time. Or at least that's what Roger says. And it better be important. The communication in the HR department is poor, but the morale is worse. The high turnover rate in staff, especially in Directors of Personnel, has put a strain within and between the departments that report to Zaco. And the Training department is definitely one of them. The most frightening thing about all this is that he doesn't see it.

Meeting him alone is also odd. I've met him twice now in three months; every time, Roger is away from the office. Given my phone call earlier with Roger, obviously it'll be another one-on-one meeting. It's a weird coincidence.

"James Treblid," Zaco says in his distinctly aristocratic tone, "It's so good to see you again. How have you been?"

"To tell you the truth, I'm a little stressed right now."

"Really? How so?"

I close the door behind me and sink into the leather wingback chair facing the perfectly clean mahogany desk. You sink so low into the seats of this guy's chairs that you can't help but look up at him. Just another one of his mind games, I'm sure.

37

I hesitate for a moment before answering but decide to be straight. "Because, sir, our trainers are very unhappy and I'm very concerned about what they might do."

"What do you believe is the problem?"

"I have some ideas, but I have a meeting scheduled with them in a few days to go over their concerns."

"What ideas do you have?"

"I think leadership is an issue."

"Are you referring to Roger's or your own?"

I didn't have the guts to tell him that it might be Roger or maybe even him, so I say, "I'm not sure yet."

"Well, keep me abreast of the matter, will you?

For the next 40 minutes, Zaco paces like a college professor and fusses with a rubber band. All the while he rambles on about the intricacies of scheduling training classes and the importance of maintaining strong relationships with our internal and external customers. Not once does he mention the trainers' workload or the dichotomy between the Sales and CS managers.

At last he sits down.

Suddenly, with no warning, he slams his fist on the desk and begins shouting. I jump inadvertently. "You have a pack of whiners working up there – prima donnas. Always bitching about something. I expect you to get control of the situation Treblid, and start making our customers happy again. I don't want to hear any more complaints from the other VPs and especially not from the goddamn President. Am I making myself crystal clear?"

Stunned by his irrational outburst, all I can say is "Yes, Sir." You could hear the capital letters.

"That will be all. Goodbye."

Next thing I know, I'm in the shops walking back to my office, wondering what the hell that was all about.

I get back to the Training department and suddenly realize that, except for Rose, the place is deserted. "Where did everybody go?"

Uncomfortably, Rose replies, "They're all in a meeting, Mr. Treblid."

"About what?" Now I'm both curious and upset.

She shrugs. It's obvious she doesn't want to say anything more.

As I walk down the corridor, I can hear voices coming from the classroom at the end of the hall. I stop. I recognize Larry's voice, "Frank and I met with Treblid this morning at about the same time you guys met Roger.

We told him that, because he was new here, he wasn't directly responsible for the shit we're in. But we also let him know he couldn't do much to help us, either; you know, he's not technical and all, which means he can't understand the pressure we feel. Let's face it, what credibility does he have?"

I walk back to my office.

Rose is sitting at her desk and by the look on her face she understands the mess we're in.

"This is not about you, James," she says softly, forgetting the formality.

"I know that, Rose." And with a devilish smile I add, "But now I know what I have to do."

"Oh?" she says surprised.

"Yup! At least I know where to start." I turn serious. "Can you pull out the personnel files of all our trainers and have them for me by tomorrow morning?"

With a concerned look, she says, "Yes, of course."

I smile and say, "Thanks. I'll see you tomorrow."

What About You? _____

- How much support (technical and non-technical) does the organization provide its employees?

  _____

  _____

  _____

- How would you describe the level of trust between people in your organization? Why?

  _____

  _____

  _____

- What are the current organizational challenges? Threats? Opportunities?

  _____

  _____

  _____

- Where is the bottleneck in your organization?

  _____

  _____

  _____

TEST YOURSELF and your SUPERVISOR

Answer each statement according to the following scale:
Almost never - 1   Sometimes - 2   Regularly - 3   Almost always - 4

7. As a manager, you're a respected
leader.   1   2   3   4

8. From your perspective, your superior
is a respected leader.   1   2   3   4

9. As a manager, you're technically
competent (...could do the job of your
subordinate competently).   1   2   3   4

10. Your superior is technically competent
(...could do your job competently).   1   2   3   4

11. As a manager, you're recognized as
someone with strong personal values
(ex. honest, hardworking, dedicated...).   1   2   3   4

12. From your perspective, your superior
is recognized as someone with strong
personal values.   1   2   3   4

13. As a manager, you have the support
of your superior for developing your
subordinates.   1   2   3   4

14. From your perspective, your superior
has the support of his/her supervisor
for developing you.   1   2   3   4

Chapter 3

The Sports Connection

Preview

James begins by revisiting his roots in Sports, which explains his passion for "coaching." He recalls the good and bad coaches he's met first-hand as Operations Manager for a professional sports team, and describes anecdotes and the lessons he learned while watching the best and the worst at work. From this introspection, he proceeds to explore and research "coaching" in business and ultimately redefines the essence of coaching for business managers. As well, James's wife, Charlene, is introduced. From the outset, it's clear that she's going to play an important role in actualizing James's coaching vision.

While the engine warms, I scrape the ice from the windows. It's not as cold as it was this morning, but I decide to let the motor run for a few moments before getting in. The cold air is refreshing and the ride home should be easy. I get into the car and begin moving towards the parking lot exit. Then I wait for an opening in traffic and abruptly make an accelerated right turn to enter the flow.

As I ease into the rhythm of the cars around me, I begin to relax. Before long my thoughts turn inward. I start thinking about my background – the last 20 years.

My confidence and focus in the area of people management began right out of university. After graduating with a Business Degree in Sports Management, I developed a curiosity for understanding people's perform-ances and the factors that affect it.

During my third-year internship, a year before my graduation, I got a first-hand look at professional sports. I spent six months working with a professional baseball team – an experience that profoundly influenced my career and got me hooked on the subject of coaching. During this time I was faced with every facet of the sport business, from promotions to operations and even a stint as an Assistant Manager for a minor league club. At the end of the internship, I returned to university to complete my final year.

Upon graduation, I began full-time with the baseball club. Within two years I was promoted to Assistant Stadium Manager. It was here that I got to meet players and managers and to learn how their relationship impacted team performance.

Russ Dravasechip was my boss and a former Major League pitcher. As the Stadium Manager for the previous four years, his management approach was pretty simple. There were no formal problem analysis or deci-sion-making processes. His management style was strictly common sense and seat-of-the-pants decision-making. But his experience and contacts in professional sports made up for the lack of business sophistication.

Russ made many friends in his career and he introduced them to me every chance he got. He was well liked by everyone, but most of all he was trusted and respected. I can't remember a home stand where the visiting manager didn't come to Russ's office to chew the fat – and the tobacco. He was on a first-name basis with every manager and virtually every player in the league.

Back in his playing days as a relief pitcher, Russ had a lot of time in the bullpen to analyze the people and the processes of baseball. He was not a superstar on the field but he took every opportunity to be a super student of the game. As a teacher he taught me more than just wins and losses but also the inner workings of the game, the teams and the relationships.

Best of all, he wasn't afraid to share his experience with a rookie like me. He loved the game and loved to talk about it. He'd go back 25 years to reminisce about a particular situation. Most of the stories were things that happened on the field with some of his teammates and off the field with some of his managers. There were some just plain funny stories too. Like the time one of his teammates called the newspaper the day after a ball game to complain to the Editor about not being given credit for a base hit in one of his at-bats. The Editor explained to the player that it was a "typographical error." The player, obviously not understanding, replied, "What do you mean 'typographical error?' Don't know who that guy is, but he wasn't even close to the play!"

He talked with great fondness about some of the managers he played for and why they were successful. He recalled one famous manager whose strategy was brilliant because of its simplicity; he'd convene the players in Spring Training and say, "Here's a ball, a glove and a bat. Now go out and play." And that was it. The tone was set for the year. He also talked about managers who weren't very good. He called them "Cavalry Generals who looked funny on a horse," the kind of managers that players didn't believe in – and it showed in the win-loss columns. He always had an anecdote to fit a situation that we were facing. For him, life and business was a metaphor for baseball and vice-versa. Together we made a pretty good team. He was an honest jock with a lot of intuition and I was the graduate with the science to formalize stadium operations.

During this period, the industry was undergoing fundamental changes. Baseball was struggling with new pressures that were threatening its profitability – free agency was pushing player salaries sky-high and the exploding media coverage was creating new revenue opportunities beyond anyone's expectations. It was the beginning of a new attitude and a new era for professional baseball; for the first time, owners had to forget the "toy" and examine the "game" as a business. The stakes were getting high and owners wanted to protect their investments. This meant replacing their "old boys" club – ex-ball players, family and friends – with professional business managers. For people like Russ, who had a passion for the game and loyalty to the owner, it meant stepping aside and taking on new duties in the organization. They moved him into a job in Community Relations and part-time Scouting. For me, it meant a promotion.

During my 10 years as Stadium Manager, I saw the effects of good and bad coaching in sports and in business. Dick Williams, "Sparky" Anderson, Buck Rogers, Tommy Lasorda, Jim Leyland and Felipe Alou were a few of the great sports managers I met and observed. I saw what made their teams successful.

I also drew from my own experience as an amateur athlete and a parent of two kids who loved sports. I had many coaches myself when I was growing up and played several team sports. I also observed many more with my children. Some were good, because they were dedicated to the kids, and some were bad because they seemed more dedicated to themselves. Derek, my son, lived a situation that should not have happened – a real-life example of bad coaching. A coach who decided to teach him a lesson shattered Derek's confidence and motivation. After he'd made front-page news in the local paper and was touted as a hockey phenomenon, this particular coach felt it was necessary to deflate his ego. The coach told me, "No one on my team should get that kind of individual attention." And from that moment on, it was a battle of egos – a young ambitious coach versus a boy with an admittedly "hot dog" attitude.

As a parent, I should have intervened, but I didn't. I know now it was a mistake. I was young myself and didn't want to be known as a problem parent, so I let the coach do what he thought was best. As it turned out, his judgment was too poor and his ego too large to make him a good coach for anyone, let alone children. This experience was a defining moment for me. It increased my resolve to understand coaching in sports as well as in business. Later, I also swore that I wouldn't let it happen again with Max or Ty.

Working in professional sports also gave me a privileged seat to view success and failure or winning and losing in a competitive environment. Sport is all business; winning was the only thing that mattered, or so it seemed. The successful coaches had a knack of getting positive results from all of their players, stars and average players alike, and this in spite of contract disputes and assorted personal problems. The good coaches took mediocre talent and transformed it into incredible performance. They also found areas of improvement for the star players; got them to buy into making the necessary adjustments and developed them into super stars. They also understood chemistry within the team and between players and managers. They had great focus. They knew when to listen, to talk, to ignore and to "kick ass." They also managed under pressure better than most coaches, whether it was pressure from the fans, media, general managers, owners, or of course the players.

They say that winning cures all ills. It's probably as true in sports as anywhere else. But what distinguishes the great coaches from their peers is their explanation for losing. With them it rarely seems a devastating event, but rather an opportunity for learning, an opportunity to motivate and an opportunity to develop skills and attitudes to succeed at a later date when the stakes were going to be higher, like the playoffs.

At the time, my interest in coaching was strictly literal. I wanted to understand what factors separate winning teams from losing teams. Needless to say, player talent is a tremendous factor, but I discovered that it wasn't usually enough.

After 10 years in sports management, I made a career change. I went back to school to do an MBA because I wanted to update my understanding of management and especially the contribution of managers in business organizations.

I spent the next five years working as a contract trainer and consultant. As a trainer for an international training group, I acquired inside knowledge of virtually every major industry, from manufacturing to financial services. Aside from instructional design, the most important lesson I learned was the value of follow-up and practice after a training session. Whether it was "Sales," "Sales Management" or "General Management," the results were the same: "no practice and follow-up" meant "no retention." Knowledge, confidence and competencies were acquired and lost, time and time again. What a waste of resources! Clients agreed with the need for practice and follow-up, but they just didn't know how to do it consistently.

I also specialized in job analyses and compensation. I learned about equity and motivation and that the absence of one usually meant the absence of the other. It was an excellent way to deepen my understanding of performance in business.

My passion for managing and coaching grew. I felt that both belonged together – whether it was on a rink, a factory floor or in a sales territory. Instinctively, the connection was clear: good and bad coaches in sports, and good and bad bosses in business have a common thread. And I was determined to find out what makes a good coach and a good boss the same.

At that moment I turn into the driveway and park next to Charlene's car.

I love coming home from work. This is where I regain my perspective on life, where my self-confidence is renewed and the day's damage gets repaired. It's where my dreams and realities converge.

As I gently close the door, I can smell the aroma of olive oil and garlic wafting from the kitchen. Love that smell.

Suddenly I hear Ty's high-pitch voice shout, "I'm first!"

Max's deeper voice shouts back, "No. I'm first!"

"Mom, tell Max that it's my turn to use the video game!"

"No way, Mom! I'm first. Ty was first yesterday!"

"Listen, you guys." I hear Charlene's husky calming voice from another room. "Work it out, or you'll both lose!"

Charlene is a great Mom." She manages a $50 million business by day and the rest of the time takes care of her family. She's just as natural sitting on Boards of Directors as she is attending parent meetings for school functions. We have a nanny, but when she's home, Charlene loves to cook. She keeps in shape, too, up at 5:30 and jogs every morning. Her blonde hair and blue eyes are an attractive cover for the awesome business sense that lies beneath. She's the most logical and practical person I've ever known. Her ability to skim information and cut to the chase is phenomenal. She's received numerous awards in her field of marketing. But despite her heavy workload, she touches base regularly with all of us and expects me to do the same.

As I walk into the kitchen, Charlene sees me and smiles. "Hi, sweetie. How was your day?"

I walk up to her and give her a kiss. "Hi yourself. The day had its ups and downs."

I grab the spoon from her and stir the sauce.

"What happened?"

I smile at her. It's nice to be home. "Let me see the kids first, change my clothes. Then let's have a glass of wine and I'll tell you all about it."

〜

After touching base with the kids and getting a report on their day, I move into the dining room where Charlene is pouring two glasses of a lovely chardonnay.

"Thanks, honey." I take a sip.

"So what happened at work?"

I tell her about my meetings with George, Frank and Larry, and my lunch with Charles; then, of course, there's Zaco's weird behaviour. I recount the frustration I feel about Roger. She listens intently and offers generous emotional support. One thing about Charlene is that even though she doesn't always agree with me, she always allows me to vent my feelings first before offering objective advice that I may not like but which usually hits the mark. After 20 minutes, I've calmed down; we talk about her day and we reverse the roles.

There aren't always crises, of course; we also share the joys and accomplishments of the day. It sounds routine to some, but for Charlene and I these moments are very precious. It makes us a strong team.

∼∼∼

Usually we go for a long walk after the kids are in bed, but tonight we're both dead tired and a good night's sleep seems more beneficial.

Before turning out the lights, I go to the den and pull out a file folder.

"Ah! Here it is!" I say.

"What's that?" Charlene asks from the bedroom.

"The paper I wrote on coaching." I say.

I turn off the light in the den and walk to the bedroom.

I begin reading.

"Coaching – An Essence Debate, by James Treblid.

Business coaching was first recognized as an important management attribute in the late 1950s. General Electric unveiled the results of an internal study in which 90% of the top managers credited a prior boss as the most important factor in their success. This finding started a ground swell of interest in the concept of coaching – a concept that originates from the world of sports.

Drawing sports concepts into business is not new. The "winning is everything" attitude borrowed from two-time Super Bowl winning Coach Vince Lombardi is wide spread in today's business world. "Scoring," "wins and losses," and "team work" are examples of sports terms that are well entrenched in today's management jargon.

Corporations are constantly inviting winning coaches to speak at business functions about peak performance and how to achieve it in business. They're asked to describe what it takes to be a winner, how to set goals and work as a team, and how to motivate and be motivated.

49

The popularity of "coaching" coincides with the growing attention to performance appraisals, mentoring programs, training and total quality management implementations. All of these activities require interaction between a supervisor and his subordinate. They all require coaching.

At the outset there are two basic issues managers face and which need to be addressed. One, there is no consensus about the business definition of coaching, and two, the causal relationship between coaching and corporate performance has not been proven – at least not empirically.

The purpose of this paper is to address these questions by first reviewing the debates that have promoted and challenged the essence of coaching. It examines the similarities and differences in the meanings given to "coaching" from three points of view: the management literature, the sport psychology literature and personal interviews conducted with winning sport coaches and trainers.

The first section reviews the evolution of coaching in management. It summarizes the positions taken by the various investigators. The second section examines the coaching issues raised in sports – the root of coaching. The third section presents the results of personal interviews with successful sport coaches. The final section summarizes the information gathered and challenges the popular definition generally ascribed to "coaching."

There are two schools of thought on coaching. First, those that believe 'coaching' is a process – a series of structured management activities that improve team performance. And second, those who view coaching as a unique management skill."

After about 10 minutes, I put down the paper and turn to Charlene. "Sports coaches and trainers are less philosophical about the subject of coaching. Unlike the academics, they make an assessment based on personal observations and experiences from repeated successful seasons. They emphasize 'respect' and 'credibility' as important ingredients to effective coaching. This isn't found in the business literature. The literature on business coaching focuses on 'skills' or 'processes.' For them, effective coaching is defined by what the manager 'does.' Sports people, however, focus not only on what the coach 'does' but also on what he 'is.' For example, a coach needs to be honest, respected, credible, hard working and a role model for others. These are values and habits that extend far beyond the process or sets of skills that characterize coaching in business."

"Isn't this what this whole exercise is about?" Charlene says.

"Yep!"

I read the next lines out loud.

"The Sports and Business debates have followed different paths. In the former, the essence of coaching is not questioned – win-loss records are what matters. Sports psychologists continue in their efforts to duplicate the perfect coach by adopting a very scientific approach to studying behaviours and personalities of winning coaches. In Business, on the other hand, there is only a strong intuitive feeling that coaching is important. In the absence of a clear definition as to what coaching is and evidence to show it is a determining factor on an organization's profitability, the term will remain a fad. In the end, Business will have only borrowed the term "coach" for the "skills" required and have left behind other critical elements that make up an effective coach."

I stop reading, put the paper down and begin telling Charlene about the discussion I had with my friend Mike and his comments about his former boss, Charles. Then it hits me. "Was this an example of a manager having the skills but not the values to be an effective coach?"

"Sure sounds like it."

"I think so. I have an idea I'm going to try out tomorrow. I'll let you know how it works."

I lean over, kiss Charlene goodnight, and turn off the lights.

What About You? _____

- What experiences have shaped the values in your organization?

  _____

  _____

  _____

- How much of your learning in life and in business was done by design and how much by chance? List your experiences:

  _____

  _____

  _____

- What lesson was learned by losing?

  _____

  _____

  _____

- What lesson was learned by winning?

  _____

  _____

  _____

- How would you define "coaching"?

  _____

  _____

  _____

TEST YOURSELF and your SUPERVISOR

Answer each statement according to the following scale:
Almost never - 1   Sometimes - 2   Regularly - 3   Almost always - 4

15. As a manager, you enjoy working
    with people.   1   2   3   4

16. From your perspective, your superior
    enjoys working with people.   1   2   3   4

17. As a manager, you consult your
    work group before making decisions.   1   2   3   4

18. From your perspective, your superior
    consults you before making decisions.   1   2   3   4

19. As a manager, you listen to what
    people tell you.   1   2   3   4

20. From your perspective, your superior
    listens to what people tell him/her.   1   2   3   4

21. In your work group, people have the
    information to adequately do their jobs.   1   2   3   4

Chapter 4

The Captain

Preview _____

James puts to the test an innovative solution to overcoming his own credibility problems with his subordinates. His conversation with Tom Wunkler is an insightful approach to bringing an unofficial group leader on side with the manager's vision. The experience spurs James on to face the daunting challenge of selling his coaching ideas to the rest of the organization.

Things are quiet in the office this morning. There's been no word from Roger regarding our meeting about the situation in the department. After looking over my paper on the coaching model, I decide I can't wait any longer. I pick up the trainers' "Personnel" files that Rose put on my desk.

I begin going through each file. Finally I come across what I'm looking for. I put away the files except one, pick up the phone and dial. After a few seconds I hear "Tom Wunkler!"

"Hi, Tom. It's James! Can you come and see me?"

"Sure, I'll be right over." His tone is friendly.

Tom Wunkler is one of the younger trainers in the department, but he's probably the biggest in size, built like a fullback. The other guys call him "Iceberg," as in "there's a lot more to Tom than meets the eye." He doesn't make a lot of noise or take up a lot of space, but his engaging smile and willingness to help others in the office sets him apart. Everyone likes him. He's usually the first to arrive in the mornings and often the last to leave at night. All in all, Tom is one of those "still-waters-run-deep" types: quiet, smart and when he talks, people listen because he's usually right. Plus he rarely seems to get too excited when the pressure is on. I like him.

I get up to greet him as he arrives. "Come on in!"

He smiles warmly as he walks by Rose. "Hey, Rose. How are you?"

You can tell she's pleased. "I'm fine, Tom. Thanks for asking."

He steps into my office.

"Can I get you a coffee?"

He settles his bulk into a chair. "Thanks."

"Regular?" I ask.

"Please."

I step out for a moment and come back with two coffees.

I sit behind my desk and look at Tom. "I looked at your personnel file and I'd like to take a few minutes to discuss your background. If it's okay?"

"That's fine," he says amiably.

"I see here that you've played a lot of team sports in your younger days."

"Yep."

"Do you still play now?"

No hint of emotion. "Yep."

"What do you play?"

"I play old-timers hockey with guys from school. The rest of the time it's with my wife and children. We like to mountain bike."

"Good for you! I also see here that you were team captain of your senior high school football and hockey teams."

"Yep." Still matter-of-fact.

"And you won a few championships along the way!"

"Yep." Now there's a hint of a smile.

I don't try to conceal my excitement. "In hockey, you won three back-to-back!"

"Yep." Now he's smiling broadly.

I pause for a moment and look at him again. "Why were your teams so damn successful?"

He gets serious; it may well be he's clued into my earnestness. "Mostly we had a good bunch of guys who could play and wanted to win."

"And you were the captain of those championship teams, weren't you?"

"Yep." Modestly.

"How were you chosen? And why?"

Pausing once again, he replies, "Each time was different. The first year, I think it was because the old captain had left – he'd graduated. I was the assistant captain, so the players figured I was as good a choice as any.

"How did you feel about that?"

"Proud. The 'C' was a nice honour. I took the responsibility seriously. And winning another championship was a lot of fun."

"So what happened the next year?"

He leans back in his chair. I can tell he was wondering what these questions were all about. "The situation was different. We had a new coach."

Without giving him a chance to elaborate, I immediately fire back, "How did that go over with your teammates?"

"It meant a new coach. They were worried."

"So what happened?"

Pausing again, he says, "This new coach was smart. One of the first things he did was call the captain, me, to get my point of view on things."

Smiling now, I ask, "What do you mean?"

He was smiling too. "Well, he was worried that the players wouldn't accept him. He wanted to know if I could help him with the players – you know, his credibility."

"And?"

"Well, I told him he'd have to earn it on his own. I didn't see how I could help."

"What did he say?"

"All he said was, 'Tom, please stay on as captain and just be there if I have to talk to the players.' I said sure."

I excitedly respond, "And you won another championship!"

"Yep."

Now he's talking without questions. "The third year was different too. Most of the players from last year had graduated, so we had a lot of new faces."

"But you still remained captain, right?"

"Yep, but mostly because I was the most senior player on the team."

"Did you have the same coach?"

He nods.

I ask, "Anything different happen?"

Still quite relaxed, he says, "Yep. It was little more work. The coach didn't have a lot of time – maybe it was patience – to work with the new players, especially the ones that needed more development. But he was good with the veteran guys and during practices he liked to work with them and have me work with the first year guys. I was like an assistant-coach."

"And you won the championship, for the third time!"

He grins hugely. "Yep."

"That's amazing, Tom!" I shake my head in admiration.

Taking a deep breath, I pause for a moment and say, "I have a special interest in sports and particularly team sports. Did I ever tell you that?"

Tom shakes his head.

"In another life I did a little research on team performance – on coaching actually. It was pretty heavy stuff. As it turned out, I found that coaching athletes is very much like coaching employees in a business. There are many similarities in the ways good teams and good work groups react to effective coaching."

"Yep. I can see that." And before I can continue, he asks, "Are you sure it's not just a 'guy' thing though?"

"What do you mean, a 'guy' thing?"

"My wife likes to tell me that women probably make better managers because they have an innate feel for managing people. They're more compassionate than men are. Maybe it comes more natural to them. I know some people don't like the sports comparison because it reminds them too much of the army – 'yes sir, no sir' – no compassion. They see pro sports coaches on television screaming at their players and wouldn't want their bosses to do the same."

"Good point." I pause for a moment. "My research, though, looked at more than just professional sports and it proved to me that effective coaching is just the opposite of the drill-sergeant types you're talking about."

I sit back in my chair and let a few moments pass.

"Tom, let me get to the main reason why I wanted to meet with you today."

I lower my head for a moment and bite my lower lip before looking up at him. "It's about my own credibility with the trainers. I need your help."

With a serious look on his face he says, "Oh?"

"Let me explain. First, do you agree that 'credibility' is about confidence in your boss?"

He ponders the question. "Sort of."

"For example, your confidence in me depends on how technically competent I am in doing my job. Which probably means I should know how to do your job too. Right?"

"I don't think it's absolutely necessary that my boss be able to do my job."

"Okay. I'm not saying it's absolutely necessary either. But what I am saying is that if the boss does have the 'technical competence' to do it, it surely helps his credibility. Don't you think?"

"In that sense, yep."

"Without credibility, I'm pretty ineffective as a manager. To be a good coach, a manager has to have more than just strong communication or organizational skills. A good coach has to be believable."

He nods.

"If a manager doesn't have it," I say, "then he's got problems. And a three-day training course on how to be credible won't solve it. It won't get me more respect, make me more honest or trustworthy, or make me a better role model. And it certainly won't instantly change the personal values I've held since childhood. Right?"

"Yep."

"Part of the answer to the problem of 'no credibility,' and you're living proof of this, is having a strong captain – someone who will compliment the coach, not substitute for him. This person is already a leader among his teammates. Not because of formal authority or his position in the organization, but because of merit. He's earned the respect of his peers. When he talks, they listen. He leads by example, not by words. Comes through in the crunch. What do you think?"

After another long pause, he looks at me with a smile. "I think there's more to this than captains and hockey. What's on your mind?"

It's my turn to crack a smile. "Tom, how would you like to be team captain of the trainers?"

Tom laughs. "I'm flattered, but a captain on a hockey team and a captain here are two different things!"

"Are they really? At the beginning of every year or season, both set goals, right?"

"Yep."

"Team performances in sports and in business are tied to these goals, right?"

He nods.

"And who takes the heat when the team isn't performing like it should? Usually the coach or the manager, right?"

He nods again.

"So for me, a sports team or this department is the same. We've got goals to reach and the coach is on the hot seat. Look, I'm not talking about the captain replacing the coach. He's got no formal authority or responsibility. I'm talking about helping the coach, or in this case, the manager. Me!"

"How do ya' see it working here?"

"Like I said, my credibility with the trainers sucks, big time!"

Tom quickly comes to my defense. "You're new here. Give yourself some time."

"That's exactly what I don't have. After what I heard yesterday, we need to move quickly. The trainers seem to respect the values I stand for, but they don't believe I can improve the present situation for them. They're growing impatient and who knows what some of them will do next. The situation is critical and I don't think I can wait any longer."

"James, there's a lot of frustration in the air right now. It doesn't have anything to do with you."

"Maybe so. But in every company things don't always work like we want them to. And every boss has to take some responsibility for it. Politics will always be part of the game, so I can't cop out here. For now, I don't have any power to make things different, but hopefully that'll change. In the meantime though, I've got to survive, and I can't do it without you."

"What do you want me to do?"

60

"If my 'technical competence' or 'dedication to the group' comes up with the trainers, I need you to show them that in spite of my shortcomings, you support what I'm doing, just like you did when your hockey coach asked you to be there for him. I need the other trainers to see and feel that you agree with what I'm doing."

I pause.

"I'll even make you a promise, Tom. Before I talk to the guys about anything that has to do with this department's operations, I'll get your opinion first. In that way, at least you and I will be in agreement every time."

He scratches the back of his head. "Does this make me management?"

I chuckle. "No. And it doesn't make you a stool pigeon either. There will be no titles, no 'C' on your shirt, no extra pay. It'll be your contribution to making the team better. It's capitalizing on the talent and skills available in the department. It's no different than how the instructors go to Frank when an electronic troubleshooting problem comes up. That's his strength. You, on the other hand, not only have technical competence but you also have good leadership skills. And even though you're not the rah-rah type, you lead by example. You'll make an outstanding manager some day – if you want to be management."

"Okay. I'll give it a shot."

I begin to relax. "Great! You know, I've called a meeting for tomorrow. I'd like to go over the agenda I prepared and get your input on a scheduling idea I have in mind. Can we meet in the morning to go over it?"

"Sure. How about for breakfast? Say 7:00 in the cafeteria?"

"Great!"

"See you then."

Tom gets up and starts to walk away. Then he turns. "I'm curious. Suppose your credibility with the trainers had been okay but the problem was something else. What would you do?"

"It depends."

Without saying a word, he nods and closes the door behind him.

〜〜

I feel better now. If my hunch is right, Tom is the perfect candidate to test my theory on "credibility." And if it works, it'll buy me some time to fix the other problems in the department – namely bottlenecks and slack.

George Pike and his foremen want the same thing my trainers and I want – a smooth process for their technicians to be trained on new products. This process needs to be predictable, efficient and reusable every time a new machine lands in our territory, because each time, the Training Department's resources are challenged and our performance is assessed. I know enough about the business to know that the process is cyclical and irregular. For every product launch the process is the same, but we don't know when it's going to happen. Could be none or two in one month. When this happens, new priorities are set and the training schedule gets overhauled. This means that before the product arrives, the Sales Group must be informed about its features and benefits and the CS Group must be trained on how to service and repair it when it breaks – because it always does sooner or later.

New machines aren't supposed to be sold and delivered before everyone's been trained, so we have a lot of pressure to deliver programs quickly – and sometimes we haven't been trained ourselves yet. It can take weeks for a trainer to learn the complexities of a new machine and develop a training program for technicians. So it's not surprising that everyone gets on our case.

Our capacity to design and deliver courses is already at its max. There's no slack whatsoever to allow for sudden fluctuations in training needs. And so our ability to turn around and deliver a new product training program isn't very good. So if we're the slowest to react to these sudden changes in priorities and we're also the last to know about them, small wonder we're looked at as the company bottleneck.

But first, let's see if I can get the trainers to believe in me.

$$\approx$$

After meeting with Tom this morning I'm anxious to start this other meeting. I look around the room and the trainers are all here. So I begin.

"Good afternoon, everyone. Like me, I'm sure you're all thinking 'Thank God it's Friday.'" They smile politely. I continue. "Thanks for being here. I know there's been a lot of frustration in the training department lately and so I would like this meeting to focus on the causes and consequences of this unhealthy situation. But before I ask you to present your views, I would like to get agreement on one thing and that is, for every issue or problem you bring up, you must also describe its impact on the performance of the department and the organization. Take a few minutes to think it through if you need to, but I think this way we're sure to have a

62

constructive dialogue. All right?"

I see nods and hear some "Uh-huhs."

I guess it's okay, so I continue. Just as I'm about to start, Tom stuns me by standing up and saying, "James, if you don't mind, I'd like to say something first." I immediately look at the people in the room. By the look on their faces, they're just as surprised as I am.

Tom begins. "I've been here for three years and there's been a lot of changes. And like everyone else, I've kept busy trying to keep up-to-date with the new technologies, adjusting to shifting schedules, bending over backwards to do customer training. Juggling all these elements has been hard." Trainers nod in support and Larry yells out, "Go get 'em, Iceberg!"

Without batting an eye, he continues. "The pressure to produce training programs is not letting up. We're all a bit tired. It's affecting our confidence and our ability to do a good job. We're all professionals and must work together to find new ways to do our business – the training business. And here's what I suggest. First, we need to define clearer goals for the department – goals that everyone can believe in. These need to be in line with what the big bosses want, but mostly they'll help us know what we should be doing and how well we're doing it. These goals should be broken down into specific objectives and activities. Each of us will be assigned a role and a goal. Each month, we'll assess how we're doing, give a little reward to those who meet the goals and make appropriate changes where we're not meeting them."

The room remains silent. Finally, one after the other, trainers nod in agreement. It's a beautiful moment. I never doubted that Tom could take charge, but to stand up and make such a powerful statement was his own initiative. I'm sure happy he has. He's playing the role of a championship captain – not for the sake of his boss, but for the sake of the team. I'm taking notes of what he says so as to leave no doubt in the minds of the trainers that I fully endorse Tom's recommendations. In his short speech, Tom captured not only the feelings but also the thoughts of the other group members and presented a solution they obviously like. I could've said the same words, but they would have sounded hollow and would have meant nothing to these guys. Coming from Tom though, there's a force behind them and the impact is profound and lasting.

After a short period of questions and answers, I ask, "Does anyone else have anything to add?"

Larry gets up. "There's something I don't understand here."

"What's that?" I ask.

"I certainly like what Tom said, but isn't it your job to be telling us these things?" A silence comes over the room.

Without the slightest hesitation, I reply, "Yes, you're right. But the situation here calls for some immediate action. And because I'm new here and don't have the technical training you guys have, I need help. I agree with Tom that we all take a role and contribute the best way we can. My role will be to promote and protect a working environment that will make this department perform at its best. I'll communicate to you what senior management wants and come back to you to discuss how we should do it. For now, I think Tom said it all; let's start by deciding what the goal of this department is, then look at what has to be done to reach it. I think we'll automatically uncover the issues and roadblocks that frustrate you and hopefully come up with some solutions that will relieve the pressure you're all feeling."

"Then let's do it." And that was the last thing Tom had to say. For the next four hours, we hammered out goals, activities and roles. It might well have been the most productive meeting I've had since arriving at MDL. And it's a wonderful feeling to know that people are happy and productive because they believe in what they're doing.

〜〜〜

I look at my watch and it's five o'clock. And yes, thank God, it's Friday!

As I look back on the events of the last couple of weeks, I realize that the meeting with the trainers was a pivotal moment. I applied an action step from the coaching model that works; having a "captain" to close the credibility gap between the trainers and myself is a temporary but effective way to begin building a foundation for deeper changes. I've seen it work in sports and more than ever, I believe it will work in business.

It's only the first step, but I feel confident now.

The time is right to press forward with the coaching model. I've convinced myself that for Machine Distribution Limited to be a great company and not just a good company, there has to be some fundamental changes in the way business is managed. The emerging technologies are pushing the learning curves of our sales people and technicians to extreme levels both in terms of quantity and speed. In order to bring about these changes, clear and consistent communications from credible and committed leaders are an absolute must. This means that a new management-employee equation is required, one where all parties must contribute. It's a step towards a so-called "learning organization" – where knowledge and competencies will be acquired from the synergy created between "leader-led training," "self-paced learning" and "coaching." I'm convinced of it.

The challenge, however, is determining the right amount of each – the right mix.

Before that, I've got to sell the coaching idea. And that's no easy task.

What About You?

- Has your credibility ever been challenged?

_____

_____

_____

- Why? What did you do?

_____

_____

_____

- Have you ever felt abandoned in a group situation? What did you do?

_____

_____

_____

continued

- Have you ever worked for someone you didn't respect?

  _____

  _____

  _____

- How did you respond? What did you learn? How did this affect your career development?

  _____

  _____

  _____

- Name 3 people who have no direct authority over you but who you consult for their advice.

  _____

  _____

  _____

- Why consult them?

  _____

  _____

  _____

TEST YOURSELF and your SUPERVISOR _____

Answer each statement according to the following scale:
Almost never - 1   Sometimes - 2   Regularly - 3   Almost always - 4

22. As a manager, you are a good role model for others.   1   2   3   4

23. Your superior is a good role model for others.   1   2   3   4

24. As a manager, you are totally dedicated to the work group.   1   2   3   4

25. From your perspective, your superior is totally dedicated to the work group.   1   2   3   4

26. As a manager, you are not afraid to discipline, if required.   1   2   3   4

27. Your superior is not afraid to discipline, if required.   1   2   3   4

28. As a manager, you tell people immediately when they do a good job.   1   2   3   4

29. Your superior tells you immediately when you do a good job.   1   2   3   4

30. As a manager you follow up with your people on a daily basis.   1   2   3   4

31. Your superior follows up with you on a daily basis.   1   2   3   4

Chapter 5

The Strategy

Preview

With the help of Charlene, a marketing specialist, James lays down a plan to get his coaching ideas known to the organization. He starts with an unusual awareness campaign to get the attention of Senior Management. He also begins to sense the forces within the company that could undermine his initiative.

"Good morning. Here's your coffee." Charlene ambles to the bed, clutching a steaming mug.

I'm groggy but grateful. "Thanks, honey." She pulls open the curtains and rays of brilliant sun bounce off walls and mirrors – quite a show.

"Well, the kids are getting dressed and will be out of here in about 10 minutes."

"Oh? Where are they going?" I ask, rubbing my eyes.

"They're spending the day with their Dad. Remember?"

"Oh yeah! I forgot."

"So I was thinking, because it's Saturday and the kids are gone all day, why don't we have a leisurely breakfast, go for a walk and catch a movie?"

"Sounds great!"

As I slip out of bed, Max and Ty come storming into the bedroom. And without so much as a "Good Morning!" it's "Bye, James, bye Mom! See you guys tonight! Kiss?" We all scramble to kiss each other and before you know it, the kids are running back downstairs. The front door slams shut and then it's silent – blissfully silent.

I turn to Charlene. "Quick shower. Meet you downstairs in 15 minutes?"

"You bet."

The fact that the kids go to their dad's every second weekend helps Charlene and I enjoy some quiet quality time together, but it's also a reminder of my role. I love the boys like they're my own, but they do have a father and I've adjusted to that. I'm the second dad, the one that fills in when their biological dad isn't around. I don't mind because the pressure is really on "dad number one"; I'm more of a big brother and a "tough" friend, especially as they get older. I know this is the role I need to play for our family to be the best it can be. The same goes for Charlene when it comes to my own kids. Even though they're in their 20s and the issues are different, her role is the same as mine – back-up for "mom number one."

When the kids are with their dad, everyone appreciates it. They get to spend some important time with their father and we get to focus on us – our relationship, goals and plans. And whatever we decide to do, we always have fun doing it.

≈

Breakfast was nice and I'm looking forward to this walk – something we do almost every day. It's a chance to exchange ideas and get some exercise.

With fresh snow on the ground and a deep blue sky as a backdrop, the sun is particularly bright this morning. During these one-hour walks we always pick one or two things to talk about. The subjects range from the kids' schooling to the national debt. Today, I decide to bring up coaching and get her advice on how to present it at MDL. My confidence and drive to push the coaching model comes from Charlene. She believes in it. As she puts it, "I truly believe your model goes beyond anything that's in the marketplace today. Coaching is more than just 'doing' something right. The model explains perfectly the profile of what a true coach should be, should have and should do. Not enough attention is given to these other dimensions of effective coaching – dimensions that make coaching a complex responsibility.

It's cold, so we walk at a brisk pace. I turn to her and say, "I need your advice."

"With what?"

"Well, it's time to get the coaching model on the corporate agenda and I need a way to launch the idea internally. Any suggestions?"

After a few moments of mulling it over, she says, "I might have one or two. Let me think out loud for a moment and ask a few questions. Okay?"

"Okay."

"The company's business plans for this fiscal year have been in place for six months. Right?"

"Right."

"And because you're midway through the first quarter, it means you won't get a formal opportunity to present new ideas for at least another six months. Right?"

"Probably."

"And from everything you've told me about this company's management style, it'd be almost impossible to get your coaching idea sold this year, especially if you follow their normal approach to new projects. Right?"

"Uh-huh."

"You've also told me that nothing gets approved unless every member of the Executive and the Operations Committee has an opportunity to assess it first. And this could take months. Not even the President will approve an idea without passing it though the formal process. Right?"

"That seems to be the case."

"And finally, the two management levels above you must approve the coaching idea before you get to present it to the Executive. Right?"

"Right. Unfortunately."

She senses my frustration. "I think I know what you have to do."

"You do?" I stop in my tracks and look at her.

She stops too. "I think so. What you have to do is take a classical marketing approach." I can sense her excitement.

"I don't understand what you mean."

"You'll have to work out the details, but I believe you have four things to do: first, define the needs of the decision makers; second, get their attention; third, offer an incentive for them to try your idea; and fourth, deliver on the promise."

"Right." I say automatically, without much enthusiasm or conviction.

"James, you might not know it but you have something market-research types spend millions trying to get."

"I do?"

"Sure! You have one important factor working in your favour."

"What's that?"

"Remember the people who first interviewed you for the job?"

"Yes."

"They all talked about the need for coaching at MDL."

"Okay."

"This means you don't have to sell them on the value of the concept – they already believe in it."

I try to hide my disappointment. "Yes, but their idea of what coaching is about isn't what my model is about!"

She stops and fires back, "So what? The important thing at this stage is that they're not against the idea of coaching. Use that to your advantage."

"How do I do that?"

"Like any marketer would – start by getting their attention. Once you have their attention we'll decide later how to differentiate your coaching model from the rest. Or as marketers like to call it – sell the added value!"

We continue, but there's no more talking.

I mull the idea over for a few minutes. "Okay. I'll think about it. It could work, I suppose." I'm not totally convinced. But the more I think about it, the more the idea is interesting.

We continue the walk without saying much. Just as we're about to arrive at the house, I get a flash. "Stop! I've got it! Let's go inside and I'll tell you about it..."

It's Sunday morning and I feel great! I like my attitude – it's positive for a change. Yesterday's talk about coaching with Charlene really got me inspired. So I'm going to the office.

For the first time in a while, I'm going to the office with a sharp focus of what needs to be done. My goal is clear and I have confidence in the plan I'm about to put in place. I feel like I'm on a mission. And I know that what I'm about to do is good for the company, good for the managers and good for the employees. It'll certainly relieve some of the pressure on the training department too.

I play back in my mind the conversation Charlene and I had on Saturday. The first step is to get buy-in by Senior Management on the unique approach I've developed for coaching effectively. The second step is to let them see the results for themselves by getting them to approve a pilot project – a low-risk approach to get results before deciding to launch the program throughout the organization. This is an approach where I can validate the model by generating empirical evidence to support my theory. For MDL, it's an opportunity to assess "coaching" in terms of a determining factor in profit making. And of course, if I can demonstrate the financial advantage of the model, then Senior Management won't be disappointed.

I need to make a business case that makes the connection clear – the model is a prescription for more profit. I need evidence that proves that training without effective coaching is almost always a waste of time and money.

I can feel my mind racing. I need to demonstrate that training as it's done now is both ineffective and inefficient. The absence of any type of follow-up is the most probable cause. I'll prove it by presenting the same case I made to George Pike – the results and comments of technicians who got three of 25 questions right. They're bound to see that training this way is an expensive exercise for people to learn and then likely forget important knowledge and skills. MDL has 500 technicians who take an average 40 hours of in-class training per year. If I use George's logic about opportunity cost being $100/hour, then I could say the company is losing around $2 million per year because of the absence of post-training coaching. That'll keep them focused.

I park in front of the building and head towards the security gate.

No one's there. I press the only button I can see and a voice says, "Yes? Can I help you?"

I say, "Yes, I'm James Treblid, Training Manager."

The voice replies, "Write your name in the log book and show me your pass." I still don't see anyone. I look for a camera and finally spot it near the ceiling. I pull out my pass and show it. The door opens and the next thing I hear is "Have a nice day!"

"You too." And I walk in.

⌇

On Sundays, the building is quiet – eerie, actually. The lights are out and nothing stirs. I walk pass the shop areas and the cafeteria and head towards the training department.

I enter the offices and without even taking off my coat or boots I immediately head for the supply room and pull out a flipchart, scotch tape, thumbtacks and a handful of markers. I go into one of the classrooms and turn on the lights.

I take off my coat and begin pushing all the tables and chairs to the side. I grab the flipchart and tear away 12 sheets. I place them on the floor side by side. Then I use adhesive tape to join each individual sheet together to form a 6-by-9-foot canvas. I stand back to take a look. It's big.

I fold the whole thing in half. The felt pens and thumbtacks go in my pocket and I begin dragging the massive sheet of paper out of the classroom and towards my office. Fortunately, there's no one around. I get to my office and fumble with my keys, finally getting the door open. I grab one corner and reach as high as I can to thumbtack it to the top of the blank wall beside my desk. I do the same with the other end. Soon the whole thing's pinned up. I step outside and look in through one of the giant windows; all I can see is white. An entire wall that used to be hospital green is now covered with this large white square of paper. Anyone walking by would have to be blind to miss it.

The adrenalin is flowing. I walk back into the office and pull out the red felt pen from my pocket. At the top centre I write in big, bold colours, "COACHING," and for the next two hours I draw the flowchart of my entire coaching model.

The "attention trap" is set! Now I've got to wait and see what happens. If I play my cards right, senior managers and especially Zaco will want to know what this is all about. With enough pressure from the lower ranks and other managers, I think he'll want to get involved if he sees a political advantage. At least I hope so.

≈

I look at my watch and it's noon. Charlene's expecting me for lunch; I quickly put away the supplies and grab my coat. Just as I'm ready to turn off the lights, the door opens. It's Charles Renacks, the Group Sales Manager – the "Asshole," as Mike called him!

"James, what are you doing here on Sunday?" And before I can answer, he looks up and frowns. "And what's this?" Not surprisingly, he's staring at the massive sheet of white paper on my wall.

I try to hide my shock at his sudden arrival. "Charles! How'd you know I was here?"

"Oh, I saw your name in the log book at the security gate."

I wave much more casually than I feel towards the model on the wall. "You want to know about this? That's just my coaching model for MDL."

"Wow! How does it work?" His tone sounds open, encouraging, but based on what Mike said, I try not to fall for it.

I take off my coat and begin explaining the model.

Charles smiles. "I'm a big believer in this kind of thing. A lot of it we already do, of course, although the terminology is different."

I sense the smug attitude, but say nothing.

He goes on, "I like it. When do you expect to have it in place?"

"I'm not sure. But I'll let you know as soon as I do."

"What does Lester think about it?" he says, fishing for some news.

"I haven't told Mr. Zaco yet."

He presses his lips together and nods.

As I turn off the lights, he asks, "Hey, can I get a copy of this? A smaller version, of course!" He laughs.

I go back to my desk, open a drawer and hand him a copy of the coaching model on a regular letter-size sheet of paper.

He walks out.

As I watch Charles leave, I think it would be a good idea to have a diary to keep a record of these visits and reactions. I might need it later to explain to the big bosses how the "coaching" idea got going.

What About You? _____

- Where do you get your ideas from?

  _____
  _____
  _____

- How do new ideas get presented in the organization?

  _____
  _____
  _____

- What are the organizational factors that affect an idea being successfully presented?

  _____
  _____
  _____

- What obstacles are usually encountered in presenting a new idea?

  _____
  _____
  _____

- How do you overcome them?

  _____
  _____
  _____

TEST YOURSELF and your SUPERVISOR

Answer each statement according to the following scale:
Almost never - 1   Sometimes - 2   Regularly - 3   Almost always - 4

32. As a manager, you are a
    good communicator.   1   2   3   4

33. Your superior is a good communicator.   1   2   3   4

34. As a manager, you know how to set
    good objectives.   1   2   3   4

35. From your perspective, your superior
    knows how to set good objectives.   1   2   3   4

36. As a manager, you generally anticipate
    problems.   1   2   3   4

37. From your perspective, your superior
    generally anticipates problems.   1   2   3   4

38. As a manager, you effectively delegate
    the workload.   1   2   3   4

39. From your perspective, your superior
    effectively delegates the workload.   1   2   3   4

Chapter 6

The Sale

Preview

As James's plan takes hold, he begins to feel the presence and pressure from his superiors. In order to move to the next stage of his plan, he develops a selling strategy to fit the individual needs of stakeholders. His first big hurdle is to sell his ideas to the manipulative Lester Zaco.

To come to the Training department all the way from the Bunker requires a good set of legs and a real desire to be here.

Two weeks have gone by and as I look through my diary, I can't help but smile at the names and comments of the managers who "happened to be walking by" my office and asked about the coaching model on the wall beside me.

February 28. Mary Giles, Warehouse Manager: "Love the concept...really like the 'captain' idea...would like my foreman to be evaluated."

March 1. Bob Regis, General Manager of the Northwest Office: Somewhat aloof, says, "My technical coordinator would benefit from such a program."

March 3. George Pike, Customer Service Manager: In his own inimitable fashion, "Holy shit! What's this?...I like it a lot, when d'we start?"

March 4. Norma Kitchell, V.P. Customer Service: Not convinced of the sports connection..."Isn't there enough testosterone in this place as it is?"

March 9. Hugh Cones, President: Was curious about the model... likes the credibility aspect of coaching...seems upbeat about the whole thing...more entertained than interested? Says, "85% of employees came in through the apprenticeship ranks and moved up the ladder here...there's been a letdown in training in recent years...we must stay on top of technology."

I read some of the other comments and put away the diary.

There's a knock at the window and I look up. It's Roger and Lester Zaco is standing there with him!

I feel the adrenalin rushing and jump to my feet. "Mr. Zaco! Roger! What a surprise! How are you?"

Zaco stares at the wall. He coughs. "Marvelous, Mr. Treblid. I've come to see what all the fuss is about."

"What fuss is that, sir?" You can't blame me for acting coy.

He snaps back, "About coaching!" He walks up to the wall and looks up and down at the model. Scratching his chin, he says, "I have one Vice President, two General Managers and now the President asking me about this coaching model of yours."

Yes! Of course, I don't say it aloud.

I look at Roger and sense his uneasiness. He's not sure what to say. He's seen it before, but at the time he didn't have any profound reaction except to say "Very interesting! Why is it so big?" I told him it was easier to explain to the trainers. He seemed okay with that. But today, I can tell he's uncomfortable.

Zaco sits down in my chair. Roger and I are still standing. Zaco starts in on me. "Mr. Treblid, this 'thing' on your wall is getting a lot of people wondering what the hell we're doing in this department!"

Roger says nothing.

Gathering my courage, I ask, "Oh? What do you mean?"

He raises his voice and stares me down. "Let me tell you what the President said to me. He said coaching is something that affects our corporate culture. And anything that affects our culture is a very serious matter. That goes for me as well! Members of the Executive Committee are asking me why they haven't been consulted about this 'coaching' thing." Pausing for a moment, he shifts his eyes towards Roger. "And because I was kept in the dark, I didn't have an answer!" He looks back at me. "The President seems to think that you don't understand our culture and that you might need a little coaching yourself."

I can feel the sarcasm and intimidation in his voice, but I don't let on. I nod calmly. "That may be so."

Ignoring my comment, he says, "Who gave you permission to take this initiative?"

Before I can answer, Roger interjects. "This is something James and I talked about. We feel it's important for the instructors to have a better understanding of their roles as coaches."

Zaco doesn't take his eyes off of me.

I jump in. "Two months ago, we did a survey of our technicians to see how much they remembered of what they learned in class here. The results were pitiful." I go on to explain how only 3 out of 25 got the right answer and how they blamed the lack of follow-up or practice as the cause – in short, they needed coaching.

As he listens to the explanation, his face softens. He runs his hand across his mouth and calmly says, "I see," then adds, "I'd like you to explain your model to me – just the major points."

I'm relieved, but before I can start explaining, he cuts me off. "Not now! This afternoon in my office, if you don't mind."

Roger clears his throat. "I'm afraid I'll be out of the office."

Zaco's voice is icy. "You don't need to be there."

Roger looks slightly shocked.

Looking back at me, Zaco says, "We'll meet at four o'clock."

"Okay."

Zaco gets up and, with Roger at his side, quickly walks through the door.

~~~

I begin to breathe normally and let the moment sink in. I feel bad for Roger, but the fact is that I finally have their attention. I'd better call Charlene.

I press on automatic dialing and within a moment Charlene picks up her private line and says, "Charlene Treblid."

"Hi dear! Guess what?"

"What! What happened?" She's excited too.

"We got their attention! Zaco just left my office and wants a presentation of the model. Your plan worked!"

"Congratulations! What's the next step?"

"Well, if we follow your strategy, the next step is to get a buy-in from each senior manager."

"How are you going to do that?"

"First, I've got to understand what makes them tick – you know, assessing their personal and professional needs. Then I'll spin the benefits of the coaching model to fit their individual needs. What do you think?"

"Sounds good. You might also want to start thinking about the incentive for them to say yes. The opportunity may come as soon as this afternoon."

"You're absolutely right. Thanks."

She adds. "Good luck! I'll see you tonight!"

"Bye, honey. I love you."

I lean back in my chair and begin thinking about my afternoon meeting with Zaco – face to face, alone, once again. The good news is that I'll only have to focus my preparation on satisfying his needs – no one else's.

~~~

To prepare for the meeting, I reach over to my bookshelf and pull out a binder on organizational behaviour from my MBA days. I look for the tab "Motivation" and then go directly to the section on Abraham Maslow and the theory of Human Motivation. Stapled to one of the sheets is a card that reads "Profiles for Managers." It's a matrix with seven columns and rows. In the first column are printed six human needs we all have: Order, Safety, Affiliation, Recognition, Achievement, Power. On the top of the other columns are empty boxes to write in the names of the people being evaluated. The purpose of the exercise is to build a selling and presentation strategy based on the personal needs of the other person. An "x" is placed in the box that intersects the manager's name and his or her primary need from the column of six. A person can have several needs but the idea is to select the predominant ones; to choose more than one or two defeats the purpose of the exercise.

I pull out a clean sheet of paper and draw the matrix. I write in "Cones," the President's name on the top of the second column. I then write in the names of the four Vice Presidents – "Zaco," "Kitchell," "Droubs" and "Foggs" – each one in his or her own box. I'm only meeting Zaco today, so I'll start with him. But first, I decide to call Roger and get his input on Zaco's personality. I figure that if I keep him in the loop he'll feel less threatened by the events, and if anyone knows Zaco, it's him. I get his answering machine, so I leave a message for him to call me. Until he does, I'll have to rely on my own perceptions and hearsay to do Zaco's profile.

From what I've seen and heard from other people, he obviously likes absolute control. I look down at the matrix and place an "x" in the box under "Zaco" that intersects with "Power." I lean back and mull over the implications of this need and how to satisfy it. I also wonder about his self-esteem – his office walls are covered with diplomas, awards, certificates and plaques that indicate someone who needs to have his accomplishments displayed and acknowledged. I put an "x" in the box for "Recognition."

After several minutes of reflection I decide that Zaco probably liked what he saw in my office. Assuming that he likes what I tell him this afternoon, I think he sees an opportunity to demonstrate his great leadership by presenting to the President an innovative project for improving organizational performance. So what I need to do is flatter his large ego and let him take charge of the project and take credit for the coaching initiative. This will at least motivate him to take the model to the next stage – a pilot-test. In a way, it sucks because he'll get all the credit. But I think it's the only way to get coaching on the corporate agenda.

～
～

As I walk into the Bunker, I look at my watch. It's exactly four o'clock. I head towards Zaco's office.

As usual all the office doors are shut and the secretaries are feverishly typing on their computers. I approach Zaco's office. Betty, his secretary, nervously looks up and says, "Good afternoon, Mr. Treblid. Mr. Zaco will be with you in a few minutes.

For some reason I'm relaxed this afternoon. And that's not usually how I feel when I meet this guy. His manipulative approach with people is anything but relaxing. I hope I haven't misjudged him – my presentation depends on it. I'll know soon enough.

Zaco's door opens and he walks out to greet me. "James! How are you?"

How pleasantly informal of him! "Fine, thanks."

I follow him into his office and shut the door behind me. He points to the conference table in the corner and we sit down. This time we're both at the same height.

He plants both elbows on the table, steeples his fingertips, smiles and leans forward. "James, it's been my intention since your arrival at MDL to let you discover and do things on your own, without my having to intercede. It's critically important for my managers to feel empowered. I don't like to interfere. But now it's time for us to work together more closely. You need to be coached on how things are done at MDL."

I nod.

Smiling again, he continues. "First, you have to understand that all management decisions start at the top. Do you know what this means?"

"I think so."

Zaco says, "Good. Roger may have neglected to tell you that before presenting any new management ideas, you must advise me first." He pauses. His voice becomes just a little louder. "Are we clear on this?"

"Yes, sir," I respond without the slightest hint of emotion. I'm not upset. In fact, I'm glad he's talking like this. It confirms my assessment – his need for power and control. It also means that if I can keep my emotions in check, I can take advantage of this later when I present the model.

"Have you signed an Employee Confidentiality Agreement?" he asks.

I'm thinking, it's to ensure that whatever come out of the coaching initiative is the intellectual property of MDL. I say, "Yes, I have."

He reaches back for a file and pulls out a sheet of paper and says, "Good. Tell me more about this model." I immediately recognize it as the coaching diagram I gave Charles Renacks the day I drew the model on the wall in my office – his initials are on the paper.

I smile amiably. "This is a unique model I developed while teaching at the University. It's the convergence of the core elements that make up an effective coach in sports and in business. It challenges the conventional wisdom about coaching – the ideas we all hear about."

"What do you mean?"

"Well, just about everything we read about on coaching deals with skills and how a good coach does things. For example, communicating with employees through interactive listening and balanced feedback, positive reinforcement and goal setting. It seems the coach's job ends with an annual performance appraisal."

I look at Zaco, but he says nothing so I go on. "I'm not saying this isn't important. It is; it's just as important as good planning, organization and delegation. But what I'm suggesting is that there are other factors that are at least as critical as these skills – factors we never hear about. This is what I mean by my model being different."

Zaco nods. Pointing to the coaching diagram, he replies, "You mean Credibility, Desire and Slack."

"Yes."

Then he asks: "What's 'slack'?"

"It's a new management term. It means more resources or capacity than strictly needed to do a specific job – extra time, money, information, space, management support and maybe even talent. Research has shown that companies obsessed with eliminating slack in their system eventually kill innovation, productivity and profitability – especially today when organizations are constantly adjusting to new forces in the marketplace. More than ever, managers need extra capacity to learn, communicate and execute the changes that need to be made. Here at MDL, the rate of technological changes is so fast and our managers are so busy trying to cope with day-to-day activities that their employees are either in the dark, behind or overwhelmed by it all. The bottom line is – our people aren't being developed."

Zaco fires back, "That's what you think?" He pauses as if to catch himself. "Maybe." He pauses again and adds, "'Slack' is a horrible expression! We'll need to change the word!"

Delighted with his need for power and control, this is where I start handing it to him. "You know best. What about 'capacity' instead of 'slack'?"

He smiles. "That's infinitely better. But I still don't quite understand what you mean by it."

"Some people view 'slack' or 'extra capacity' as a bad thing. But it's like cholesterol – sometimes it's good and sometimes it's bad. The same applies to 'slack'. Trying to eliminate all the 'extra capacity' in a system is probably futile and certainly fatal."

Zaco doesn't react.

I think he's locked into the model now, so I go on. "Too much capacity is as bad as not enough. Do you remember the old 'Lucy Show'?"

He nods.

"Lucy is working on an assembly line in a chocolate factory. Her job is to take chocolates off a conveyor belt, wrap them individually and place them back on the belt. At first, the flow of chocolates is slow and so she easily keeps pace. But when the number of chocolates starts to increase she can't keep pace and begins to panic. Instead of letting the unwrapped chocolates flow through, she begins frantically stuffing them in her blouse and mouth. It was a very funny episode."

Zaco isn't amused. "James, I have a meeting in an hour. What's your point here?"

I think to myself, shut up Jim-boy, you're talking too much. "Sorry. The point is this – having extra capacity in a system is not automatically bad. Because if there's no extra capacity or 'slack' in the system, how can it manage an unforeseen surge in demand? We'd do like Lucy and instead of delivering finished goods, we'd end up stockpiling – stuffing things anywhere we can."

"Hmm! Interesting idea. We still need to change the word. I'll decide later."

With the slightest of grins, I nod.

"Tell me more about the other factors."

I go on to present the rest of the model without Zaco saying much. I discuss how each manager is evaluated, the analysis process and the prescribed action steps – where the model becomes especially powerful. He has some reservations, but overall, he likes it.

And then bang! "When can we be ready to present this to the President?"

I can't hold back my grin. "I could put a presentation together by next week."

"Good. You'll show it to me first. And I'll make the necessary modifications. Let's meet here next Tuesday at the same time. I'll set up a meeting with the President for Thursday. So be ready!"

It's hard to hold back my enthusiasm. "That's great, Mr. Zaco! Do you want me to tell Roger about it?"

He shakes his head. "No. We'll work on this together. Roger doesn't have to be involved. I'll tell him."

I'm not surprised. "Okay."

I get up from the conference table and walk out without looking back.

〜〜〜

As I head towards the Training department, I feel a little tight. I'm thrilled at the idea of finally getting the opportunity to present the coaching model. At the same time I'm apprehensive about how it's going to feel when I finally present it.

Presenting to the President is going to take more than glitz. Everyone tells me he's an extremely meticulous person – obsessed with details. I wonder where he fits into the personality matrix? Low risk-taker maybe? Need for safety? That would make sense. This means minimizing the risk of this project and showing the upside. It also means downplaying the fact that the model is unproved and promoting the advantages of a pilot project. I'd better be prepared to answer all types of questions relating to concept, execution, logistics and of course costs.

I'll think about this again later. For now I need to concentrate on getting buy-in from Zaco. He's the key to getting to Cones and the other members of the Executive.

What About You? _____

- Think of a situation where you needed to get a message through to the rest of the organization – what happened?

  _____

  _____

  _____

- Before presenting a case, what type of analysis of your audience do you do?

  _____

  _____

  _____

- How emotional do you get with your new ideas? What happens when they get criticized?

  _____

  _____

  _____

- Has a manager ever told you, "I don't have time..." What was your reaction?

  _____

  _____

  _____

TEST YOURSELF and your SUPERVISOR

Answer each statement according to the following scale:
Almost never - 1   Sometimes - 2   Regularly - 3   Almost always - 4

40. In your work group, policies and
    procedures are clear.   1   2   3   4

41. As a manager, you get along well
    with others.   1   2   3   4

42. From your perspective, your superior
    gets along well with others.   1   2   3   4

43. As a manager, you require that new
    skills be practiced.   1   2   3   4

44. Your superior requires that new
    skills be practiced.   1   2   3   4

Chapter 7

The Model

Preview _____

James explains the basic premise for the coaching model, its architecture and how it's applied in practice. He's careful to acknowledge Zaco's input, especially because he's counting on him to champion the project up the corporate ladder. In the process, he discovers that another senior manager is out to derail the project.

Hope I've got everything. God only knows a week to prepare was more than enough; I've been living with this model for years. I feel my heart pumping and remind myself that the tactic with Zaco is to leave enough holes in the presentation so that he sees them and fills them with his own ideas. This'll satisfy his ego and need for control, give him some incentive to take ownership of the project and push it through the Executive this year.

I arrive at his office and he's giving instructions to his secretary. He sees me and waves me into his office.

"Okay James, let's see your presentation."

Without saying a word, I enter his office and set up my laptop to the slide presentation; I also give a hard copy to Zaco. I can feel his impatience and decide to cut the small talk and get right into it. "If it's okay with you, I'd like to show you each slide and have you make corrections as we go along." Corrections. He'll love that.

"That's fine. Let's start."

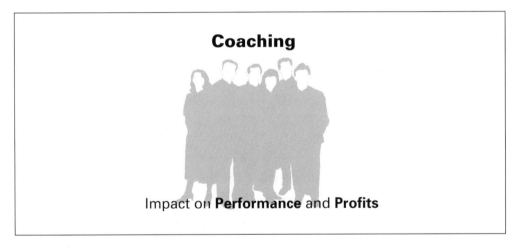

I begin. "The key to the success of this project is to demonstrate the strong relationship between effective coaching, employee performance and company profits – a relationship grounded in scientific evidence, not hearsay or anecdotes. Our purpose is to get approval for a pilot project in order to gather enough evidence to measure the correlation between these outcomes and to disprove that effective coaching is based on skills alone."

Zaco interjects. "No. I don't like that. Let's change it." He takes a felt pen and writes on the hard copy that I gave him: "Our objective is to increase corporate profits through improved employee performance."

I'm thinking to myself, "Great! He's starting to take ownership." Out loud I say, "Yes. That's better."

I go on. "The next thing is to present the current situation in training. Here are three slides that explain the symptoms, problems and probable causes."

Analysis

Symptom 1
Skills learned
in training classes
are not being used

Problem
No follow-up
after training

Causes
> Roles are not clear
> Managers don't feel
  like it
> Managers don't know
  how to do it
> Managers don't have
  time to do it

Zaco perks up. "I like this slide. It confirms what I've been saying now for several years – especially the point about not knowing how to follow-up."

I go to the next slide. "The second symptom we observed is that the employees cannot keep pace with the rate of all the changes in technology."

Analysis

Symptom 2
Employees cannot
keep pace with the
rate of change in
new technologies

Problem
Training department
cannot meet
demand of ops
department

Causes
> Traditional training
  methods are
  inadequate
> Inadequate
  resources (time,
  personnel)

Zaco adds "Yes that's true!"

And before I can continue, he adds loudly "And not only that, our top performers are burning out! They end up doing most of the technical work because the managers don't know how to get the other guys up to speed. We need a slide for that, James."

I feel he's taking control now and as long as he doesn't tamper with the essence of the model, I'll agree with his ideas – enthusiastically, of course. "You're absolutely right!" I say with conviction. "Take a look at this next slide."

Analysis

Symptom 3
The high-performance employees are getting tired

>

Problem
High performers get called upon more often

>

Causes
> Managers don't have the resources to develop other employees
> Managers don't have confidence in other employees

Zaco responds, "That's good. I'll think about it some more and let you know what needs to be changed."

Dandy! I go on. "It's clear that technology is pushing MDL to change its approach to training employees. The system as it now exists isn't doing the job. If we don't change, we'll lose our competitive advantage and our leadership position. And we can't let that happen."

Zaco doesn't miss a beat. "And we won't!"

I present the next slide.

Recommendation

V

Change the traditional training approach

He purses his lips. "We need to work on this one. Make it more complete. Show the consequences of not changing our ways."

Thinking of George Pike's argument of $100 per hour plus the million dollars in direct costs we already spend, I reply "No problem. I'll put together a graph showing the opportunity costs associated with ineffective training."

The man is hooked now!

I show him the next two slides in rapid succession.

How?

 Forge a new partnership between the training department, line management and the employee

< Decrease in-class learning
< Increase self-learning opportunities
< Increase on-the-job learning opportunities **(Coaching)**

On-the-job Learning
by Manager / Coach

In-class Learning
by Training Department

Self-Learning
by Employee

"The rest of the presentation will focus on the coaching model – a critical element of 'change' management."

Coaching Model

History

> Sport connection

< Management connection

<> Convergence of Sport and Management

"To begin, let me explain where the model comes from.

"First, an exhaustive review of both the sport psychology and business management literature was undertaken. This was followed by personal interviews with very successful professional sport coaches and/or their trainers. From these sources, a list of key characteristics describing effective coaching was drawn and analyzed. The analysis revealed that the characteristics could easily be placed into three distinct dimensions of what a coach IS, what a coach DOES and what a coach HAS. Further analysis revealed that, in practical terms, these three dimensions of 'effective coaching' came from: Credibility, Desire, Skills and Capacity." I pause and wait for a reaction from Zaco.

He steeples his fingers but says nothing.

I continue. "The model engages organizations to ask four basic questions about their managers' abilities to coach effectively: Does the manager have credibility? If not, what actions need to be taken? Does the manager have the desire to coach? If not, what actions need to be taken? Does the manager have the skills? If not, what actions need to be taken? Does the manager have the capacity? If not what actions need to be taken?"

I pause again – still no reaction. I take a deep breath and continue. "In order to make it a useful business tool, I designed several practical instruments to help organizations discover and apply the power within the model – assessment survey to evaluate a manager's coaching profile, computerized analysis of the profile and action steps are some of the instruments."

"For example, the assessment survey and analysis will reveal a manager's coaching profile by organizing the information according to the four principal factors of the model – Credibility, Desire, Skill and Capacity. Action steps are taken if the manager's scores are below a pre-established standard. For instance, if any of the questions relating to the manager's 'credibility' are equal to or below the 2.5 rating, they are extracted and tagged as 'Opportunities for Improvement.' Even if only one characteristic relating to 'credibility' is below the acceptable score, then the answer to the question 'is the manager credible?' must be 'no' and actions need to be taken to address the situation."

Zaco interrupts. "Hold on Treblid! You lost me! Where does the 2.5 rating come from?"

"Each of the 45 questions in the assessment survey is linked to one of the 33 characteristics defined by the coaching model. The ratings for each characteristic are based on answers ranging from 1 to 4 with the higher score being favourable. Average scores are determined for each question or characteristic. The '2.5 rating' has been arbitrarily set as the minimum acceptable score; any characteristic with an average score below 2.5 should be looked at more closely." I pause for a moment and ask, "Does this make it clearer?"

"Okay. I get it. What happens next?"

"You can't go on to the next factor, 'desire to,' until the question of 'credibility' is either answered by a 'yes' or by initiating specific actions to resolve the underlying causes of a 'no.'"

Zaco's getting impatient. "I don't understand."

"The premise here is that if someone isn't credible, no matter how motivated or skillful they are, they'll be ineffective with their subordinates. So it makes no sense to go forward in the process until a satisfactory solution has been found."

"What do you do then?"

I go on, "Well, it's not obvious. I think you'll agree that training is not the answer – not even the best training will instantly make someone credible."

Zaco nods.

I say, "Take a look a this slide."

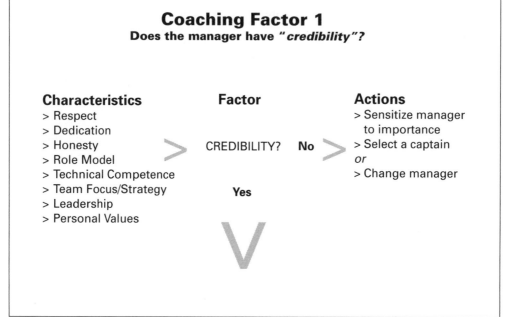

"There are two actions recommended here – and they're not mutually exclusive. First, through an 'Awakening Process,' sensitize the manager to the importance of credibility and specifically to the features that are perceived as deficient. This could be done by reading about the topic and participating in a discussion to understand the merits of these characteristics and their impact on credibility. One topic that would be covered is Ethics and its benefits to management. If professional competency is an issue then technical development programs would also be recommended."

"Second, the manager may opt to select one or several people in his work group who are considered informal leaders and would be credible among their peers. This person will be assigned a role of team captain. Captains are a compliment to the manager, not a substitute. They have no formal authority or organizational status, but like in sports, their influence on team members is felt. The captain's public support of the coach translates into team support for the coach. In the short term, the presence of a captain will minimize the credibility gap between the manager and his subordinates and allow the manager some time to improve his methods and knowledge base, and in time earn the credibility of his subordinates. Once the manager's credibility is established, the need for a group captain decreases."

Zaco can't resist. "Wait a minute. Why would the boss be credible with the 'captain' and not the other subordinates? If he's not credible with them, why would your 'captain' support him?"

"Good question. Let me try to explain it by going back to my own experience here at MDL. Do you remember when I was hired, the discussion we had about product knowledge?"

Zaco shrugs.

I go on. "We talked about my abilities in instructional design being one of the key competencies required for the job. Product knowledge was not a requirement."

He nods.

"It didn't take me long to see that with our group of trainers I had a real problem – a credibility problem."

"What do you mean?"

"These trainers have very strong technical backgrounds. They have many years of service with the company and understand the learning challenges facing our technicians. For their boss to be weak in these areas is difficult to accept."

"So?"

"After the first couple of months it was obvious that even though they seemed to like me as a person, they didn't have confidence in me as a boss."

"How would you know something like that?"

"Two of them came to my office and said it straight to my face."

"Who?"

"Doesn't matter who. What's important is what happened afterwards."

I can see that Zaco is annoyed with my answer but he doesn't interrupt.

I continue. "I decided to use the coaching model on myself and evaluate my profile. I realized that my credibility was low, especially in the area of technical competence, and no matter how hard I tried I wasn't going to change the situation quickly. So I decided to find a 'captain' to help me."

"How did you do that?"

"I selected the person that I felt was already viewed as an informal leader among the instructors – someone whose technical abilities were admired by his peers. I sat down with him to explain the situation. I said to him that, given the low morale in the department, using his natural leadership and technical abilities in a more public manner could make a huge difference to our climate. I talked in terms of 'personal contribution' -- using skills he came by naturally and was respected for. I asked him to play a more visible role in the department to demonstrate publicly his support for what I was trying to do. He agreed to be the captain with no strings attached, that is, without a title or more money or special status. In fact, as far as his peers are concerned, the only perceptible difference is that the captain will openly support the coach – something he didn't do before. What I did promise the captain though, is that from that moment on I was going to get his input into strategic plans for the training department before making public announcements. He liked that – felt that I valued his opinion. I must add though, that if he'd thought I was a schmuck, he could've politely declined, but I do have some redeeming qualities that he and the others appreciate."

Zaco can't help himself. "Who is it?"

"Tom Wunkler."

"Wunkler? I don't know if he's ever said more than two words around me. Are you sure?"

"That's why they call him 'Iceberg.' There's a lot more below the surface than meets the eye. Since Tom has agreed to be the captain, you can't believe how much difference it has made in the department. The trainers have a new attitude towards their job and their boss. Tom took on a leadership role after I convinced him that this would be his contribution to the training team. The guys trust him and listen to him. It takes nothing away from me as their manager. In fact it takes pressure off me to know all the technical stuff. We still have a long way to go in the department to overcome the bottlenecks we're creating in the system, but at least now our trainers are motivated to make some changes."

Zaco grins. "You've got a crutch!"

I smile back and say "Yeah, maybe a small one. But it's only for a short time. I need the support to continue to manage effectively. Without the trainers' confidence, I'm not going to survive the changes that I think need to be made. In the meantime, I'm doubling my learning of the business, the technology, the culture and the challenges of technical training. Already I feel there's better communication between the trainers and myself."

Zaco nods shortly. "Okay, it could make sense. Will your 'Pilot Project' prove this?"

"I believe it will. And if it doesn't, we'll at least have confined the investment to a sample of the organization, not the whole population."

"That's right." There's a pause and Zaco asks, "Any other options if 'credibility' is low?"

"Changing the manager." I reply. "It could happen that the manager refuses to accept the results of the questionnaire and doesn't want to participate in the "Awakening Process" or identify potential captains from his subordinates. Or, as you've said, maybe no one will want to be his captain – too self-serving, untrustworthy, core values or personality traits that subordinates can't tolerate in a boss. In these extreme cases, the manager should be replaced."

Zaco fires back, "Hold on here! We're not going to do that in the pilot project, are we?"

I reply, "No. To change the manager is really a last resort. For the pilot project, we'll just have to find managers who are willing to cooperate and try the action steps prescribed."

He seems relieved. "Okay. I think it could work. Now, assuming we can get past 'credibility,' what's next?"

"As you know, many managers are credible – recognized for their leadership, respected by peers and subordinates alike. People in their environment constantly seek their opinions. Right?"

Zaco nods.

"The problem here is that some of them prefer to keep a low profile. They don't usually take initiatives that might upset the status quo. It happens especially if they've been in their jobs for many years and aren't interested in change. What this means is that in spite of their credibility, they have no desire to challenge and develop their people – something effective coaches must want to do."

"And I suppose that training a supervisor to be motivated isn't the answer. Right?"

"Right. The reason managers don't want to coach is usually that they don't have the time. Others say they don't know 'how' or even 'what for'? and 'what's in it for me'?"

"If not training, then what?"

Coaching Factor 2
Does the manager have the *"desire to"* coach?

Characteristics	Factor	Actions
> Discipline		> Evaluate motivation and reward system,
> Firmness		
> Individual Attention	DESIRE TO...? **No**	> Evaluate the amount of capacity in the position,
> Flexibility		
> Feedback/Evaluation		
> Personal Development	**Yes**	> Negotiate for rewards and slack with boss *or*
> Relates to Others		> Select a captain

"As this slide shows, if the 'desire to' coach is absent, the supervisor's reward system needs to be reviewed – in other words, the rewards that incite the supervisor to want to develop his subordinates. The action step here is to investigate with the supervisor why he doesn't have the desire to coach – sometimes it's money, sometimes it's recognition and sometimes it's just ignorance; that is, he or she doesn't know how to coach his or her people. Most supervisors won't attempt an intervention if they're not confident in doing it. Sometimes it's all of the above. The research that I have done shows that the absence of appropriate incentives or resources is at the root of the lack of motivation."

"Clearly, if people feel underpaid, unappreciated and unrecognized for their efforts to develop subordinates, the desire to coach will be less. To correct the situation, an in-depth and honest evaluation of the compensation structure is required."

"It's also true that if they feel swamped with work and don't have the 'slack' or capacity to adequately develop their people, they won't. We'll see later how to overcome this dilemma and resolve the 'capacity' problem."

Zaco checks his watch. "Okay, so after 'Credibility' and 'Desire to

Coach,' what's the next factor?"

"The third principal factor is the set of skills a supervisor must possess to develop his people. As described in the model, skills are either 'task' or 'people' oriented. The action-steps to overcome skill deficiencies are training based."

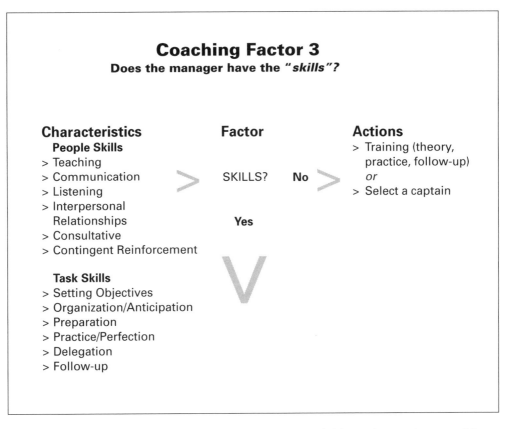

Coaching Factor 3
Does the manager have the *"skills"*?

Characteristics	Factor	Actions
People Skills		> Training (theory, practice, follow-up)
> Teaching		
> Communication	SKILLS? No	*or*
> Listening		> Select a captain
> Interpersonal Relationships	**Yes**	
> Consultative		
> Contingent Reinforcement		
Task Skills		
> Setting Objectives		
> Organization/Anticipation		
> Preparation		
> Practice/Perfection		
> Delegation		
> Follow-up		

"There are many training programs available in the market to address the 12 basic coaching skills identified by the model. The key to skill acquisition is to give training on a need-only basis; that is, supervisors receive training that is specific to them. No one is subject to generic training, the conventional approach where all supervisors get the same training. Follow-up to training is also essential. This means testing for retention and ensuring that practice opportunities to perfect the newly acquired skills are established."

"Most Training Consultants start and end with skills training for managers, believing that if a manager knows how to do it, behaviours will automatically change. There's no denying that skills are important, but as you've seen here, what you're going to be presenting to the President on Thursday is unique – no one else in the marketplace offers it. It goes well beyond the traditional 'skills-only' approach."

"We'll test several training programs during the pilot project to see which ones are best suited for our type of business and environment."

Zaco interjects impatiently. "Let's move on to the next factor. We'll cover the details of the training programs when we meet with the President."

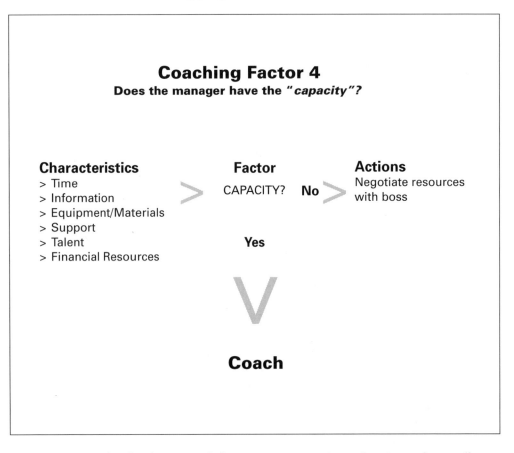

Coaching Factor 4
Does the manager have the *"capacity"*?

Characteristics
> Time
> Information
> Equipment/Materials
> Support
> Talent
> Financial Resources

Factor
CAPACITY? **No**

Yes

Actions
Negotiate resources with boss

Coach

"Sure. The final principal factor is 'capacity' – what I used to call 'slack.'"

Zaco cringes at the word but says nothing.

"This emerging management concept is fundamental to effective coaching. Without the extra capacity to innovate and develop subordinates, a manager's credibility, desire and skills will not be enough to produce an effective coach."

"What's the action step here?"

"There are two. First, the manager reviews activities that make up the processes in his department and are supposed to lead to the company's ultimate goal – making money. Second, learning how to sell and negotiate. This is a set of skills to help a manager systematically plan and present a compelling case for more 'capacity.' This action step calls for a customized sales and negotiations training program. The program will teach supervisors a proven way to link 'capacity' to organizational needs. It'll also help supervisors overcome objections through an intelligent exercise that ensures a fair and shared commitment on the part of the supervisor and his boss. Obviously, it won't always work, but why not give the manager a process in which he at least gives the proposal every chance to succeed?"

Zaco cuts me off. "I think you're going to have difficulty selling this one. I can hear the other VPs saying 'You've got to be kidding. Every manager wants more slack.' They'll use it as an excuse for not coaching."

"Remember that capacity is the fourth and last factor in the model. It's examined only after the first three factors have been addressed and satisfactory action steps agreed to. Also, keep in mind that this is a pilot project. So on a small scale, we can test this idea without committing a lot of resources."

"That's true," agrees Zaco.

"Finally," I add, "the entire evaluation process and action steps could take several weeks to complete. But once it's done, management must ensure that appropriate follow-up by the coaches takes place. Tests and post-training interviews are a must. This means evaluating coaches for their knowledge and competency retention every month for at least six months following each action step. Tests, case studies and role-plays are useful devices to validate retention and skill transference. This is the commitment we as an organization must be prepared to make."

"Six month follow-up. Okay, I can see that, but who's going to do all this?"

"Me. Remember, it's a pilot project. I'll coordinate the entire thing because some steps might require some fine-tuning."

I show the next slide. "This shows the whole 'coaching' model – the process and its elements."

Coaching

The Standard Profile		Sources

The Standard Profile **Sources**

> Respect
> Dedication
> Honesty
> Role Model
> Technical Competence
> Team Focus/Strategy
> Leadership
> Personal Values

> Interviews
> Surveys
(Person, group, supervisor)

> Discipline
> Firmness
> Individual Attention
> Flexibility
> Feedback/Evaluation
> Personal Development
> Relates to Others

> Interviews
> Surveys
(Person, group, supervisor)

> Teaching
> Communication
> Listening
> Interpersonal Relationships
> Consultative
> Contingent Reinforcement
> Setting Objectives
> Organization/Anticipation
> Preparation
> Practice/Perfection
> Delegation
> Follow-up

> Tests
> Surveys
(Person, group, supervisor)

> Time
> Information
> Equipment/Materials
> Support
> Talent
> Financial Resources

> Interviews
> Surveys
(Person, group, supervisor)

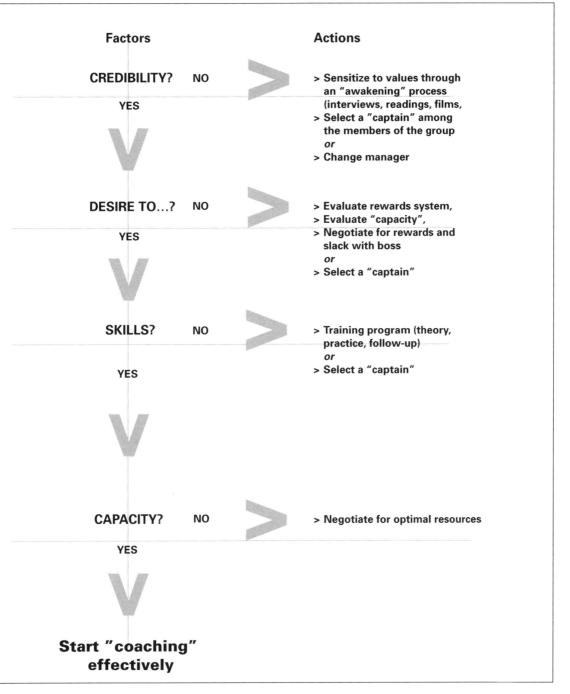

Factors

Actions

CREDIBILITY?   NO

> Sensitize to values through an "awakening" process (interviews, readings, films,
> Select a "captain" among the members of the group
> *or*
> Change manager

YES

DESIRE TO...?   NO

> Evaluate rewards system,
> Evaluate "capacity",
> Negotiate for rewards and slack with boss
> *or*
> Select a "captain"

YES

SKILLS?   NO

> Training program (theory, practice, follow-up)
> *or*
> Select a "captain"

YES

CAPACITY?   NO

> Negotiate for optimal resources

YES

Start "coaching" effectively

"The next slide describes the measures we are going to use to determine if the model is effective."

Performance Indicators:

> Organizational climate

> Image (department)

> Productivity (department)

> Profitability (department)

Measuring Devices:

> Organizational surveys:
  "Employee Satisfaction Survey"
  "Organizational Climate Survey"

> Employee performance appraisal

> Departmental profit/loss statements

> Coaching surveys and interviews

"As you can see, the four performance indicators to be measured before and after the pilot project are the department's climate, image, productivity and profitability. And the instruments used will be surveys, performance appraisals, profit and loss statements and interviews."

I continue. "The next slide describes the steps in the project."

But before I can put it up, there's a knock on the door and it flies open. It's the VP of Customer Service, Norma Kitchell, and she looks mad as hell. She's waving a copy of the coaching model in her hands. So I'm thinking to myself, "Oh boy! This is going to be ugly." I sit back in my chair, anticipating a fight.

Kitchell is furious. She turns to me and says, "James, will you excuse us for a few minutes?"

I leap out of my chair and head towards the door.

Even the closed door couldn't conceal the angry words that followed. "Lester! Is it true that you're presenting this 'coaching' thing to Cones on Thursday?"

Zaco calmly but forcedly replies, "Norma, I know your meeting with Hugh has been bumped but..."

Kitchell's tirade cuts him off. "Look, I know that you and Droubs are all high on this coaching stuff. But dammit, I'm responsible for meeting profit targets on the service side and I know very well that what we need are better business processes and not some jock-based management training. Lester, I don't know what you've got on Cones, but we've already agreed to a business plan for this year, remember? So please, get in line and drop this 'coaching' thing! Alright?"

There's no response.

Kitchell continues. "Jeez! How can you guys bring this up now?"

Still no answer.

I then hear Zaco say – and visualizing his grin. "Norma, I understand your frustration about getting the business processes revised. I also understand that you're upset at having 'coaching' introduced midstream and ahead of your project. But Hugh feels it's important."

Before she can say anything Zaco adds, "It's not a done deal, so get the bee out of your bonnet! Why don't you sit in on my presentation Thursday?"

"Are you kidding? I've already told Hugh I'd be there. And so is Droubs!"

Feeling like a fly on the wall, I'm thinking, "Well, James, you wanted some attention and you're getting it – big time. You've got the President, Hugh Cones, the VP of Sales, Hank Droubs, VP of Customer Service, Norma Kitchell, and the VP of Human Resources, Lester Zaco. Not bad! The only one who's still missing is Jerry Foggs, the VP of Finance."

Just as the thought crosses my mind, I hear Kitchell blurt out, "And so is Foggs!" She storms out of the office and glares at Zaco and snaps, "You better be ready to get shot down, Lester, because nothing is going to derail my project!" As she stomps by me, she's so mad I'm not sure if she even cared that I was there. If she did, it didn't show. I look up back at Zaco standing in the doorway.

He smiles – it's the kind of smile you'd expect from a gunslinger who's looking forward to a showdown. Finally, he says, "Screw her!" Then he adds, "Okay, where were we? Let's keep going."

What About You?

- Have you always been enthusiastic about the training you were scheduled to receive? Why or why not?

  _____

  _____

  _____

- Identify the 3 best and worst training programs you have ever received. Explain why.

  _____

  _____

  _____

  _____

- How are training requirements determined in your organization?

  _____

  _____

  _____

- What training would you like your superior to take? Why?

  _____

  _____

  _____

- Is your superior motivated to coach you? Why or why not?

  _____

  _____

  _____

continued

- How many managers do you know who are NOT in Sales (and are not planning on being in Sales) and have taken sales and negotiation training as part of their development?

  _____

  _____

  _____

- How are projects prioritized in your organization?

  _____

  _____

  _____

- What event would change the order of priority?

  _____

  _____

  _____

TEST YOURSELF and your SUPERVISOR

Answer each statement according to the following scale:
Almost never - 1   Sometimes - 2   Regularly - 3   Almost always - 4

45. As a manager, you are a good teacher.   1   2   3   4

46. Your superior is a good teacher.   1   2   3   4

47. As a manager, you are always
    well prepared.   1   2   3   4

48. From your perspective, your superior
    is always well prepared.   1   2   3   4

Chapter 8

The Pilot

Preview

Zaco and James present the coaching model to the Executive
Committee. Because of some important opposition to the
coaching project, James counters with one of Charlene's ideas for
defending his position and dealing with the situation. James also
meets with the managers who will be involved in the pilot
project. Using easy-to-understand examples and language, James
explains the parameters and logistics for the pilot project.

With a full moon shining, the yard and driveway are as bright as can be. There's nothing like a brisk walk around the neighbourhood to clear the mind and get a little exercise.

Just as I turn the corner at the end of the driveway, I hear a honk. It's Charlene. She couldn't be home for dinner, so this was my first chance to tell her how it went with Zaco.

"Hi!" she says as she steps out of her car. "Give me a minute to change. I want to go with you…"

I give her a kiss and say, "I'll wait for you."

A few minutes later she's running out of the house, fighting with the zipper on her coat. She finally puts on her gloves and we're ready to go.

We immediately pick up a good pace and she asks, "Well, how'd it go?"

I look at her. "Things are moving fast. Very fast!"

"Oh?"

"I'm presenting the model to the entire Executive Committee on Thursday, the day after tomorrow. To everybody – not just the President."

"That's wonderful, isn't it?" she asks.

I measure my words. "Yes and no. Zaco seems ready to take over the project and sell it to the President. That's good. But during my meeting with him this afternoon, Kitchell, the VP of Customer Service stormed into his office and threw a major conniption. She was furious with Zaco's attempt to squeeze the 'coaching' project on the Executive agenda ahead of her 'business processes' project, especially since the 'coaching' project was never in the plans for this year. She even implied that Zaco was holding something over the President's head – like blackmail or something."

"How did Zaco react?"

"He didn't, except for a smirk when Kitchell left the office."

"So what's the fallout to all this?"

"Kitchell has threatened to kill the project."

"What do you mean?"

"She wants her 'process' project to go first and will do whatever is necessary to make it happen."

Charlene says, "You know, that's not so bad. Could be worse!"

"How could it be worse?" I fire back.

"You've got an edge on her, James."

"What do you mean – an edge?"

Still calm, she says, "She's told you her objection!"

"So what?"

"She's told you her objection," she repeats. Then she adds, "And you haven't even presented your case yet. Don't you see? She's told you what she wants. So what you have to do is give her what she wants – without giving up your pilot project."

Puzzled, I ask, "How do I do that?"

"Do you remember a couple of months ago when Max asked you about getting him a snowboard?"

"Yeah."

"Do you remember what you said to him?"

I hesitate. "Sort of. I think I said no because it was too expensive."

"Right," she says and adds, "Didn't you increase his allowance lately?"

"Yes, so what? We made a deal."

"Oh? What kind of deal?"

"We agreed that if he did additional chores I'd pay him extra. But that had nothing to do with the snowboard. We talked about the extra allowance several weeks later."

"That's true. But what you don't know is after you said no, Max asked me if there was any way you'd change your mind about the snowboard."

"And you told him to do more chores?" I said sarcastically.

"No, silly. I told him that if he wanted to change your mind he should find a way to overcome your objection. He came up with the idea to do more work for more cash on his own – and show you he could pay for it himself. He'll probably come back to you in the next couple of weeks with his counterproposal."

"Hmm! Pretty smart. He's lucky he's got a marketing expert as a mother!"

Charlene continues, "Kitchell has a problem with timing. Right?"

"More like she's got a different set of priorities."

"Okay. Do you agree it's because she feels her 'process' problems should be addressed before the 'coaching' problems? And her objection isn't because she thinks coaching is less important but rather because it's less urgent, at least in her mind, right?"

"You may be right."

Smiling now, she says, "Show her how both projects can be done at the same time without jeopardizing either one. And I'll bet you the 'coaching' project stays afloat!"

I put my arm around her and give her a hug.

～～

I walk into the boardroom and two of the Vice Presidents are already there. Jerry Foggs from Finance and Rob Droubs from Sales are talking about sports. I say good morning and move immediately to the front to set up my laptop presentation.

"Good morning, everyone!" I look up and it's Cones, the President. Right behind him is Kitchell. They both sit down.

"Mr. Treblid," Cones starts. "While we're waiting for Mr. Zaco, I'd like to get your view on the management training here."

I wasn't expecting the question. "Well, sir, as it is with all our training, the absence of post-training follow-up is definitely a negative factor."

"What do you mean?"

"If managers, like technicians or sales people, don't practice or have someone help them apply what they've learned in a training class, then it impacts negatively on customers and ultimately on MDL profit."

"Give me a break!" Kitchell charges back. "Are you trying to tell us that because our people aren't being coached the right way at the right time, our bottom line is at risk?"

I respond calmly. "When it comes to products and processes, that seems to be the case." I pause for an instant and add "But now we have to prove it!"

Kitchell doesn't try to hide her sarcasm. "And how are you going to do that?"

At the same time, Zaco walks in and says, "That's what I'm going to present to you this morning."

He comes to the head of the table and immediately starts into the presentation. I sit down.

～～

I look at my watch and think to myself – 45 minutes and the presentation is going well. We've made it through the 'Situation Analysis' and the 'Model.' The next step is for Zaco to recommend the pilot project. Then it's up to me to present the methodology.

I tune into Zaco's closing comments.

"...So as I've shown here, a pilot project will minimize our risk by limiting the initial investment in the program. It'll give us the opportunity to determine the value of this coaching model. Any questions?"

Foggs asks, "Lester, how much are we talking about here?"

Zaco responds, "It depends. I suggest we let Mr. Treblid present the particulars of the pilot project first and then discuss the costs at that time."

Kitchell blurts out "Forget the costs. The question is when! It's not part of the business plan because we agreed the priority this year was going to be placed on processes, not people management. Right, Hugh?"

Cones half nods.

Before Zaco can answer, I stand up. "Ms. Kitchell, you're concerned that the coaching project will take place before yours, right?"

She's obviously surprised by my question. She looks at Zaco and says, "Not only before but against my project."

"Do you recall when Mr. Zaco presented the third factor of the coaching model – 'Skills'?"

She stares at me and says nothing.

"Do you agree that setting objectives, organizing the work flow and anticipating bottlenecks are important elements in determining efficient and effective processes towards greater profitability?"

"So?"

Feeling my pulse racing, I continue. "In the pilot project, the managers are required to examine their processes before doing anything else." I pause for a moment. "The examination is not as exhaustive as what you had in mind for your project, but I believe it's a good first step towards your goal." I pause again and add, "I'd like to show it to you." I look at Zaco and sense his discomfort with this, but he doesn't say anything.

I go on. "It's a one-day training program in which managers review their goals and processes. The basic premise is that MDL's goal is to make money. And anything that impedes the flow of resources towards achieving this goal should be re-evaluated, re-designed and if necessary removed from the system. It's a first attempt at streamlining operations. And that includes removing inefficient managers who unknowingly create bottlenecks in the system. I think that with a minimum of coordination, we can run both projects, yours and the coaching project, simultaneously – as compliments to one another. If you like I'll send you a complete outline of the program."

I look at Zaco, then at the President. They're both trying hard not to smile. Kitchell shrugs and says nothing more.

I look at Zaco again and ask, "Should I continue?" Both he and the President nod.

"I'd like to present the methodology for the pilot project so that we can see the level of commitment required by all parties."

Pilot Project — Steps

> Select 2 groups ('test' and 'control')
  within each of the 4 divisions
> Evaluate managers in each group
  (180 degree survey)
> Analyze results of survey
> Decide on action steps for 'test' group (only)
> Follow-up for 6 months
> Re-survey each group again
> Compare results with 1st survey
> Conclude if 'coaching' made a significant
  difference
> Make decision on roll-out

"The first step is to define the groups that are going to be involved. We've selected two managers from four divisions: Welding, Sales, Warehousing and Service. In each division, there'll be a designated 'Test Group' and a 'Control Group.' This means there will be in total four 'Test Groups' and four 'Control Groups.'"

"The second step is to have all eight managers evaluated. The data collected would compare a manager's coaching profile to that of the ideal coach – the standard established in the research. It compares the manager's profile against the best. It involves gathering the perceptions of the manager, his subordinates and his superior. They answer the same 45-question survey. Once all three parties complete the questionnaire, average scores are determined and action steps are decided. The third step is to..."

Cones looks at Zaco and interjects, "Mr. Treblid, I don't think we need to go through all the details of the project here. What's the bottom line to your proposal?"

"For now, what we need is the commitment of various stakeholders. Let me show you my last slide."

Commitment

Senior Management:
Approval of pilot project demonstrates management commitment to employee development

Line Management:
Allow 30 min. for each group to be surveyed and again in 6 months for the 2nd survey (If some results are not clear, a focus group will be formed to review results)

Allow 5 days of training (average) and 1 day of follow-up per month, for 6 months for each manager (coach) of 'test' group

Coordinator:
Allow 1 week for survey, logistics, questionnaire; 1 week for evaluations; 4 weeks for training; 1 day per month for follow-up; 1 week to collect and analyze data from 2nd survey; 1/2 day to present findings

---

Droubs, the Vice President of Marketing, asks, "Do we really need a pilot project? This stuff looks pretty solid. Why wait? Let's go ahead now!"

Before I can reply, Zaco says, "Yes, it looks good in theory, but let's not be too hasty and make the same mistakes we've made in the past. Do you recall the disaster we suffered with our last management program? The one where managers were told to respect each other's space – or put differently, their area of responsibility? It was a disaster. Especially when one of the managers told Ms. Kitchell to 'get out of his airspace'! Remember, Norma?"

"How can I forget? I wanted to fire the guy on the spot!"

"So let's be cautious and do our homework first. We'll come back to you with the results of the pilot project in six months. We'll be ready then to assess the impact of the model and decide if we should put 'coaching' into next year's Business Plan."

Everyone nods in agreement – including Kitchell.

Zaco then adds, "Do you want to talk about the project with your General Managers before making a decision on the pilot?"

"What the hell for?" says Droubs. "They're the ones who told us about this coaching idea in the first place. I don't know why they'd object to a pilot project, especially since the time investment is rather nominal. What do you guys think?"

Kitchell: "I don't have any problem with the pilot idea and my GMs aren't going to buck either. Like you said, they're the ones who brought it up in the first place."

They all nod in agreement.

Cones looks at Zaco and says, "Good luck!"

"Thank you." Zaco is actually smiling.

He looks at me and gives me the signal to leave. Without saying another word, I close the laptop, gather my notes, give a last look at Zaco and walk out of the room.

I realize that I have to act quickly and meet with the managers who are going to provide two supervisors to participate in the pilot project. I hurry back to the office and pick up the phone to schedule an afternoon meeting.

~~~

"Good afternoon, everyone! Thanks for being here on such short notice." I look around the room. There's George Pike, the Customer Service Manager, Charles Renacks, the Group Sales Manager, Mary Giles, the Warehouse Manager, and Al Varis the Welding Manager.

Except for Varis, I've met all the others before. I know George's intensity and drive for profit margins. I know I've got to watch out for Renacks – he may have a hidden agenda. Mary is a joker but she shoots straight; she's not afraid to give her point of view or to ask questions when she doesn't understand something.

From what I've heard, Varis is more sullen. There's talk about his Division being re-organized and so his attitude is less than positive. When I talked to him to set up this meeting though, he seemed fine.

I continue with the introduction. "As I told you over the phone, the Executive has given me a green light to go ahead with a pilot project to assess a unique 'coaching' idea that most of you have already heard about. What I'd like to do this afternoon is make the same presentation I made to the Executive this morning and then lay out the specifics for implementation. Any questions or comments before I start?"

"Yes" says Varis. "James, you must have some kind of pull around here, man!"

"Why do you say that Al?"

"To get the bosses to accept this thing midstream is quite an achievement!"

I shake my head. "Well, not really. As you'll see, it's only a pilot project, so the organization's total investment and risk isn't that great. But thanks for the thought!"

I present the first slide of my presentation and begin explaining the model.

As I reach the point in the presentation where the President had asked me to wrap it up earlier, I just keep going. "What I'd like to do now is walk you through the steps of the pilot project."

"The first thing is to select eight supervisors from four different divisions that'll participate in the project. And in order to ensure that we're comparing apples to apples, it's critical that we choose two supervisors from the same division."

Mary Giles, the Warehouse Manager interjects. "It's a cool idea, James, but there's something I don't get. Why two supervisors from the same division – why not just one?"

"And why the hell do we need four divisions in the first place?" fires off George Pike. "Might be a fancy project for you, and a damn good one, but you've got to understand, Jimmy Boy, that for me it means more costs – meetings, training and whatever other goodies you've got in mind to take away my supers from their jobs. Geez – you know they've got plenty to do as it is. Besides, what the hell are we running here anyway – a business or a goddamn lab?"

"Okay George, I see your point. Let me explain why we need the four divisions and eight supervisors." I pause for a moment. "The first thing to remember is that we want to validate the model before eventually rolling it out throughout the company. That means using a sample size large enough to make the findings significant and at the same time minimizing the investment in time and money. Wouldn't you feel more confident about putting all your supervisors through the program if the pilot project proved that your people are better managers with 'coaching' than without it? And when I say 'better,' I mean a better bottom line for your department."

"Sure, James, but what happens if my guy fails?" asks Charles Renacks.

"Well, let me put it to you this way. First, my hope is that the pilot project will show that, for the trial period, one of your people did better than the other. And hopefully it's the same person who we put through the 'coaching' process. Second, if the trial is inconclusive or fails to show performance gains with one of your sales managers, than we should review why it didn't work in your department and seriously consider excluding your department from the roll-out. The purpose of the pilot project is to make sure we don't paint all the managers in the company with the same brush. This way, the investment for each division can be contained to the pilot project. If it doesn't work for you in the pilot project then you don't have to participate in the roll-out."

They all nod in agreement.

"Getting back to Mary's question though, the reason for having two supervisors from the same division is to provide consistency and reliability in the results. Let me explain what I mean. You'll agree that each one of your areas is subject to environmental forces that are specific to itself; a supervisor in one department often faces pressures that are different in timing and magnitude than those faced by a supervisor in another. The Welding supervisor and the Sales managers don't wrestle with the same issues, right? So to make sure that we compare performances with similar circumstances, at least two subjects must be from the same department. It's like testing row boats."

"What?" Charles practically snarls.

"If you've got four rowboats and you want to know which one's the fastest, how would you do it? Would you put a rower in each one, line him up in the water, and whoever wins the race has the fastest rowboat?"

He shakes his head. "Come on James, of course not! If it's the rowboat you're evaluating, you have to have the same guy row all four! Otherwise, you might end up selecting a bathtub."

"You're right! How would you evaluate the best rower then?"

"Have 'em all row the same boat, of course," replies Charles.

"Right! And what I'm saying is that in our pilot project we're going to evaluate them first, train only half of them and then evaluate how they perform under four kinds of sea conditions, so to speak. The purpose of the exercise is to determine if the 'training' made a difference in the performances and under different circumstances."

"So how do we do that exactly?" asks Mary.

"Like they do in medicine!"

"What do you mean?" asks George.

"How do you think doctors determine what treatment to prescribe a patient suffering from some ailment?"

"Take two of these and call me in the morning!" bursts out Mary. They all laugh.

I smile. "Two of what, though? That's the heart of the matter, isn't it? How do they know it's going to work? They rely on scientific evidence that assures them that under certain circumstances, one thing leads to another – a certain pill leads to a certain reaction that leads to a certain healthy outcome. Right?"

"Jimmy, you're losing us here. What the hell are you talking about?" George sounds impatient.

"Let me explain in another way. The 'coaching' idea is too important to leave to chance and the only way I can prove that my 'coaching model' works is to have one supervisor go through the coaching process and the other supervisor in the same department not go through the process. I then gather the right quantity and quality of evidence to demonstrate that 'coaching' made a difference, and if repeated, the results would be the same. You know, the ability to predict with a certain level of confidence that something will occur if something else does." I pause for a moment and ask, "If two of your supervisors had a headache and you gave an aspirin to one and a placebo to the other, and found out that 9 times out of 10 the person who took the aspirin felt better then the other person, what would you conclude? That aspirin works! Right?"

Charles says, "So you want four supervisors from four different departments to be the 'test' group – the people who take the aspirin, so to speak. And you want four other people, from the same departments to be the 'control' group, the placebo-takers, so to speak. Then you're going to evaluate each supervisor before and after you've given them their 'pills.' And if the 'aspirin' people get relief from their headache and the others don't, you'll conclude that it's because of the aspirin. Is that about it?"

"That's pretty close. Obviously, the pilot project will not be assessing headaches – instead it'll evaluate climate, image, credibility, desire to coach, skills, capacity, productivity and profitability where possible. And the aspirin we're going to give is called 'coaching.' Some will get it and some won't. After six months we'll reassess. If a difference between the 'test' group and 'control' group emerges, we'll be claiming, with a probability greater than 50-50, that 'coaching' improves performance. But let's be realistic. Don't expect to see a 25% improvement. I'd be very happy with 5%. Can you imagine if all our supervisors and managers improved their department's individual performance by 5%? What it would mean for the company's profitability? It would be dramatic!"

"Maybe even a bonus!" blurts out Mary.

Everyone laughs.

I ask, "Are we okay on this point?"

"I get it now," says Al.

The others seem to get it too.

"And before you ask, 'How are we going to get this information?' I've designed an assessment questionnaire that each subordinate from each of the eight supervisors must complete. The supervisor completes the same questionnaire and so does his boss – meaning you people. Figure on 30 minutes to do it. Also be certain that the entire group does it at the same time. It's important that the answers be spontaneous. It makes for more honest answers."

I show them the questionnaire. After a few minutes, Charles asks, "At the beginning of the questionnaire you write, 'From your perspective, blah, blah.' What do mean by 'perspective'?"

"It means that even if the respondents are not absolutely certain of the right answer, they should go with their feelings, intuition or perspective of what they think is reality. It's important that each question be answered. Remember, the subordinates, the boss and the supervisors complete the same questionnaire. We'll be getting information from three different perspectives. And what we're looking for are trends and variances."

"Here he goes again! What does that mean?" Mary groans.

I walk over to a blackboard and as I'm writing I say, "Okay. Okay. I'm sorry. Let me show you. Let's suppose I've got you guys reporting to me. You all complete the questionnaire to assess my performance. Remember that a score of '1' means 'never,' '2' means 'sometimes,' '3' means 'regularly,' and '4' means 'almost always.' Here's a sampling of the results.

	Al	George	Charles	Mary	AVE (Grp)	StDev	James	Roger	AVE (Roger & I)
#45	4	4	4	4	4.0	0.0	3	3	3.0
#31	2	3	3	4	3.0	0.8	2	3	2.5
#32	1	1	4	4	2.5	1.7	1	4	2.5
#13	1	1	1	2	1.3	0.5	3	4	3.5

For Question #45 – 'The supervisor is a good teacher,' you all gave me a score of '4.' In other words you think I'm a good teacher 'almost always'; my boss and I assess my ability as 'regularly' – still pretty good. From these scores I could conclude that 'teaching' is not a problem for me – the high average of '4.0' and '0.0' deviation indicates a high score with no variance.

For Question #13 – 'support from the boss,' Al, George and Charles all give me a '1' – 'almost never' – and Mary gives me a '2' – 'sometimes.' What does this mean?" I ask.

Mary says, "It means that you don't get much support from your boss, at least from their perspective. Right?"

"Right. And what else do you see?"

"Your boss, Roger, doesn't have the same perspective. He puts down '4' and everyone else '1's, '2's or '3's. Looks to me that there's a communication problem," says Al.

"You might be right. One thing is certain; I should investigate further in order to explain the wide difference of opinion between my boss and everyone else.

"So," I continue, "What about Question #32?"

"Woah! Big difference of opinion among the crew on this one!" Mary says.

"Yes, but the average score isn't that bad!" says Charles.

"You're both right." I respond. "The 'Average' says it's not bad but when you look at the deviation, which statisticians call 'variance,' you're left with some questions. The 'Average' score alone is not enough to explain the overall appreciation of the matter – the degree of unanimity is also an important factor. We'll discuss it again later.

"Let me try to summarize what we've said here. The assumption is that, given the scale of '1' to '4,' an 'Average' score of '2.5' or less on any of the questions is arbitrarily deemed as being low and therefore represents an opportunity for improvement. In other words, because all the questions are linked to a specific characteristic of effective coaching, the low scores indicate which areas of coaching the supervisors need to address and improve."

"We also have to reconcile major differences between the 'Average' of the group and the 'Average' score of the supervisor's self-evaluation and that of his or her boss. For example, in Question #13 the group average score is '1.3' while the other average score for Roger and I is '3.5' – a significant difference of opinion or perspective regarding the matter of 'support from the boss.' A subsequent interview with the supervisor and, if necessary, with some of the subordinates, is required to clarify the matter. These interviews are an attempt to explain the difference of perspective and reach a consensus on a new score. If the new score is still below the minimum required, the matter remains an opportunity for improvement."

"Finally, standard deviations will also be determined. This measure will describe the variance in opinion among the group of subordinates. It tells us how much they all agree with the average score. For example, they might all agree with the average score or they might be split down the middle, indicating the existence of two factions within the same work group. Like question #32 seems to tell us."

"Sorry, James, but can you run that by me one more time?" asks Mary.

"Sure. I'll try to be clearer this time. Remember, earlier I said there are a lot of ways to get the same average. For example, a set of scores of '1,2,3,4,' '1,1,4,4,' '3,3,3,1,' or '2,2,3,3' all have the same average of '2.5.' But as you can see, just because they have the same average doesn't mean they all mean the same thing. In fact, these sets of scores suggest totally different interpretations. The set of '1,1,4,4' suggests an important split among the members of the group being surveyed, while the set of '2,2,3,3' indicate the group is reasonably close to a consensus on the question – they all pretty much agree on the same score. This kind of information is very useful in understanding the true extent of a supervisor's appreciation by all his people. If we just relied on 'Averages' to explain the results of the 45 questions, we could be missing some important stuff. What do you think?"

They all seem to get it and nod in agreement.

"We'll use something called 'Standard Deviation' as the measure of spread and have some guidelines for interpreting it. We'll say that a 'Standard Deviation' between '0' and '0.5' is a concentrated opinion, where everyone pretty much shares the same perception. A standard deviation between '0.5' and '0.8' will be considered mixed or evenly spread – perception is scattered and there's no real consensus. Finally, a standard deviation greater than '0.8' will be judged as a major split, where there is serious polarization of perceptions – in other words, where the views are obviously opposite to one another." I look up to check that they're still with me. "Does this make sense?"

"It's a bit fuzzy, but I'm sure you'll explain it again when we get to the real thing," says George. He adds, "So what's next?"

"Next is to get the names of the supervisors and decide in which group to put them – the 'test' group or the 'control' group. I'll meet with them individually to explain the pilot project. From there we'll set a date for the group surveys. Afterwards, the supervisors and you will also complete the questionnaire. Once the questionnaires are in, I'll tabulate the results and meet each 'test group' supervisor to show them."

"Are we going to be able to see the results?" asks Charles.

"That'll depend on each supervisor. I'm sure you understand that for the purpose of the pilot project, if we're going to get honest answers and the full cooperation of the supervisors and their people, they've got to feel comfortable that they're not going to get hounded by you people because of low scores, at least not immediately. The supervisor, however, will have the option of showing you the results if he so chooses."

"How much time are they going to be in training?" asks George.

"That too will depend on the results of the survey. For the supervisors in the 'control' group, it's none; and for those in the 'test' group it'll range from none to 10 days. And by the way, training is not the only action step. Remember that training is not the solution to everything. And also remember that for two hours every month I'll follow-up with each 'test' group supervisor to verify how he or she's doing. I'll also test them for knowledge and competencies – reminders to help them apply what they've learned from the 'coaching' process to their jobs.

"Any other questions?"

They shake their heads.

"Okay, can you give me the names of the supervisors you want in the project?"

"Sure." says George. "Put down Ben Amber and Don Brit as my guys."

"Amber!" shouts Al. "You've got to be kidding, George! How can you choose him? He's just a miserable son of a bitch – a warhorse. Out of touch with today's world. He's so set in his ways that no one is going to change him. You know that! What are you trying to do? Deliberately sabotage this project?"

George's face is red with rage and he blasts back, "You're not exactly a fresh daisy yourself, Al, so back off! Amber's my guy. It's my call and you don't have to like it! Okay? Besides, if this project can do anything with Ben, then I'll be sold on the 'coaching' project."

Al says nothing.

Pretending to ignore the outburst, I turn to Al and ask, "What about you, Al, who are you putting on the program?"

"Barry Lake and Joe Yatch."

"I want Brenda 'Peach' Astrim and Rich 'Rose Bud' Pillow for our group, James," says Mary, trying to lighten the mood of the room.

"What about you, Charles?" I ask.

"I'd like Dan Wetomy to be one of them. How would you feel if I was the other?" There's a pause.

"Hmm. Do you want to be in the 'test' group or the 'control' group?"

"Put me in the 'control' group."

"I hope you understand that you'll be evaluating each other's coaching effectiveness?"

"I don't have a problem with that."

"Okay then. I'll call each one of these people after you've told them about the project and set up a time and place to meet them. I'll also ask them for a date to survey their people. All right?"

Everyone agrees.

What About You?

- What are the critical success factors for implementing a management training program in your organization?

  _____

  _____

  _____

- Can you think of a management training program that failed in your organization? Why?

  _____

  _____

  _____

TEST YOURSELF and your SUPERVISOR

Answer each statement according to the following scale:
Almost never - 1   Sometimes - 2   Regularly - 3   Almost always - 4

49. As a manager, you organize the work assignments well.   1   2   3   4

50. From your perspective, your superior organizes work assignments well.   1   2   3   4

51. As a manager, you're not afraid of being flexible, if required.   1   2   3   4

52. Your superior is not afraid of being flexible, if required.   1   2   3   4

Chapter 9

The Evaluation

Preview _____

James faces serious resistance to participation in the pilot project. He must convince at least one veteran supervisor of the value of the program for both the company and the supervisor. But James learns of an internal plot to unseat him from the coaching project that will test the limits of his resolve to see the project through.

"Hi!" I wave Ben Amber into my office.

As he stands arrow straight in the doorway, the brush cut, steely eyes and compact build give him the look of a Marine Sergeant. "Good afternoon, Mr. Treblid," he says, and sits down.

Ben has a reputation as a tough supervisor. 'Mr. Personality' he isn't; and it didn't matter to him. A lot of people didn't like him. But it was easy to see why George Pike, his boss, did – he got the job done and made money too. He was intense and drove his technicians hard, not hesitating to cut into their weekends and pressuring them to do overtime.

He'd recently been transferred from the Hydraulics Section to take on the bigger job of Foreman of General Services. With a crew of 10 men and 2 women, he'd be responsible for repairing loaders, excavators and paving equipment. Many of the employees reporting to him weren't happy with the move and were looking for transfers elsewhere in the company – obviously, not a healthy situation.

I say "Sit down, Ben. I want to show you something."

I close the door behind him and walk over to the 'coaching' model on my office wall. "Have you ever seen this?"

He focuses on the image. "George sort of showed it to me," he says dryly.

"Good. I've met with all the other test group supervisors in the pilot project. You're the last on the list. What I'd like to do is show you the model in more detail and tell you about your role in this project. Okay?"

He doesn't even try to fake enthusiasm. "Sure."

"Well, what do you think?"

He shakes his head and curls a lip. "In other words, we're guinea pigs."

"What do you mean?" I say, startled by the contempt in his voice.

"You're new here, right?"

"It's been several months now. Why?"

"Do you know how many times we've been forced to accept new hotshot management ideas that were going to revolutionize our business?"

I shake my head.

"I've been here a lot of years and I've stopped counting the times," he says. "As soon as a new fad pops up, someone in the Bunker thinks it'll solve our problems on the floor. Listen, I'm not saying that your research isn't any good, but to tell you the truth I don't follow sports very closely. Besides, from what I hear, sports coaches get fired a lot."

"Yes, that's right. And do you know why?"

He shrugs.

"The life span of a professional sports coach with a struggling team is very short – inexorably short. What I mean is that there is no flexibility here – it's win or get out. Corporate sponsors, media coverage and fans put a lot of pressure on a team's ownership to make changes if the team doesn't win. If they're not getting their money's worth, changing the coach or manager is the usual knee-jerk reaction."

Ben doesn't react.

"I must admit, though, that some sports teams carry this 'coaching change' tradition a bit too far. For example, have you ever heard of Billy Martin – used to manage the New York Yankees?"

"Wasn't he the guy who was fired and hired back a couple of times?"

"Yeah. Five times, as a matter of fact."

He smiles. "Hmm…"

I feel Ben relaxing a bit. "That was an exceptional case. The reality in professional sports is that because of the outside pressure, coaches are prime targets for blame – scapegoats, you might say, if the team doesn't do well. Can you imagine the turnover we'd see with business managers if they were subject to the same kind of pressures and exposure?"

"Mr. Treblid, I understand what you're saying, but our business isn't sports. So where's the connection?"

"You're right, selling and fixing heavy equipment isn't like professional sports. But what I found is that managing a group of people in any business is very similar to managing a sports team. For example, didn't you agree earlier that the principal attributes of an effective coach apply to your job as a foreman?"

"Sort of." He pauses for a moment, and as if to catch himself, says, "You might be right, but quite frankly the only reason I'm here today is because George told me to be. So just tell me what you want me to do."

I'm disappointed but I try not to let it show. "Okay, Ben, I hear you. Thanks for being honest with me. I think I can appreciate your point of view – no one likes to be used. But I'll make you a promise: if after this discussion you still feel uncomfortable with this project, you can opt out. Okay?"

"Right." says Amber sarcastically.

I ignore his tone. "Look. This is a pilot project. It'll succeed or fail because of two reasons: one, the soundness of the model, and two, the motivation of participants like you. If you're forced to be in it, the entire project is jeopardized. And I'm not going to let that happen. I'll take every precaution to make sure it works. So the last thing I want is to have people in the pilot who don't want to be there."

"Sure" he says, not totally convinced.

"Let me add one more thing. If it were left up to some senior managers, there wouldn't be a pilot project at all – they would just as soon roll this thing out to the entire company immediately. But I said no. And Ben, you'll have to take my word for it, but I also told them I wouldn't roll it out without making sure it had a chance to work in this organization. And I meant long term."

I sense him softening and I repeat: "I mean it, if you don't want to do it, you don't have to. Okay?"

Somewhat reassured, he says "Okay, thanks. Tell me some more about the program and how it's going to work. I'll decide later if I'm going to continue."

"Fair enough." I proceed to explain the steps of the program. I explain the confidentiality of the results and how the findings will be presented.

At the end he says, "James, I'm from the old school. I believe in 'an honest day's pay for an honest day's work.' There're a lot of guys in the shops who aren't pulling their weight. You've got no idea how hard it is to get people to work overtime. Some sneak out by the back to make sure they don't see me at the end of the day – afraid I might ask them to work longer. You know, in the old days, everyone wanted overtime! I guess they don't need the money as badly today."

"You're right, times have changed."

He smiles grimly. "And I know that. But dammit, so have our customers. They don't want to know about our problems. They just want their machines up and running as quickly as possible. Their livelihood depends on it. They squeeze us because their own customers are squeezing them to get the job done as cheaply as possible, and on time!"

"You're right, but you can't do it alone – you need your employees' help. And you know as well as I do that coercion isn't the answer. Sure, managers today have to be more bottom-line driven, but at the same time they've got to understand that people aren't machines to be turned on and off whenever the boss says so."

Ben shrugs.

"Let me tell you a true story to illustrate my point. Forty years ago, my dad almost lost his job as a shift-boss at the mine he worked at. Why? Because he refused to live on site in the company's housing project. He and my mom felt it was necessary to have a life in the local community, outside of the work environment. And not only that, they also had the audacity to build a summer cottage on a lake two hours away from the mine – this was unheard of for a mine employee, let alone a supervisor. Did it have a bad effect on his career? Maybe – but over the next 25 years he went on to become Mining General Foreman, the second highest position in the largest mine in the area. Not bad for a guy with elementary education who lived off-site, with a summer cottage. I'm told he drove his men very hard, but with common sense and compassion. At least that's what they said about him."

"His boss, on the other hand, the same guy who almost fired him earlier in his career, lived on the mining site. And believe it or not, from Monday to Friday he'd sleep in his den, with whatever documents he might need during the night, in case something came up at the mine. On week-ends he'd join his wife in the bedroom. Is that dedication to the job or what?"

"Where did he end up?" Ben asks, obviously interested.

"He became Mine Superintendent, the biggest job in the mine."

Ben smiles.

"But that's not the end of the story. In his late 50s and after 40 years of loyal service, the company forced him into early retirement. He wasn't ready. Because of his single-minded dedication to his work, he had no outside interests and was bored to death. In fact, a few years after retiring, he died of a massive heart attack. The irony, though, is that after he retired, he and my dad remained friends and he'd visit us regularly at the cottage."

Ben frowns.

I continue. "My dad taught me, before I learned about it in management books, that everyone needs balance in their lives – including employees. And this means that managers must be sensitive to their people's needs, their goals and their feelings. Things like motivation, teamwork and recognition are more than just fancy words from academic cone heads. People have a life after work and they want to be treated with respect. Like you said earlier, throwing money at them to do overtime doesn't work anymore."

"So what am I supposed to do – let them run the shop?" Ben snaps back.

"No. What I'm saying is that if your guys don't perform, it doesn't matter what the reasons are; you're the one in the hot seat. And like they say in sports, 'It's a lot easier to replace the coach than all the players.' I think the same is true in business, unfortunately. Rightly or wrongly, it's the easiest solution. What do you think?"

"I see your point." Ben says resignedly.

"There's good news though. The coaching evaluation we're asking your people, your boss and yourself to complete in the pilot project will be a first step in getting a picture of how you look to them right now. And, if necessary, what you might want to do to improve it."

"You've got to be kidding! These guys are going to kill me. Do you have any idea what my reputation is in the shops?"

I try to reassure him. "They might score you low. But you know what – that's the challenge, the challenge of winning in a situation that seems impossible. If the coaching program can contribute positively, even just a little to your department's performance, it'll be because you worked at it. And both management and your employees will recognize your commitment to improve. If the performance doesn't change, or worse, if it drops, then the coaching program will take the hit and it'll disappear from your department. So what have you got to lose?"

"I see your point," he says. "My reputation can't be much worse than it is now." He gets up from his chair and walks up to the 'Coaching Model.' He turns around to look at me. "So when do you want to do the evaluations?"

"I've met with the other foreman of your department, Don Brit, and he told me if it's okay with you, we could have both your crews come in and do the evaluations this afternoon around 3:30. I know it's short notice, but do you think we could do it then?"

He barely hesitates. "Sure. This way we'll get it over with quickly!"

"Have your people come up here and I'll fill them in on what to do. I'll have the results by tomorrow. Do you want to meet at the same time tomorrow to go over them?"

He nods and walks out of the office.

~~~

As he leaves the department, I notice that Rose is visibly upset about something. "Is everything okay, Rose?"

She shakes her head angrily. "No."

"What's wrong?"

"James, did you know that Lester Zaco records telephone conversations?"

"What?"

Waving a tape at me, she says, "This. This is a tape recording of a conversation between Roger and him!"

"Where did you get that?"

"In the inter-office mail."

"From who?'

"Don't know."

"What's it about?"

"You'd better listen to it!"

She hands me the tape. "That bastard! This is illegal!" she says bitterly.

I hurry back to my office and close the door. I pull out a small tape recorder and insert the tape. After I press 'Play,' the first voice I hear is Zaco's,

"Roger, what do you think about Treblid and the 'coaching' project so far?"

Roger's voice responds clearly.

"Sounds like everything is moving along okay. James tells me that the evaluations are almost all done and that he'll be ready to meet the supervisors again next week to give them their individual results."

"That's not what I meant. I'm receiving complaints from quite a few managers that Treblid is being too aggressive with his project."

"Oh? Who?"

"That's not important. It seems that Treblid is not being a very good team player. Managers are asking him for training and he's been telling them that training may not be the right solution to their problems and that they should wait until the coaching program is in place – or something along those lines. Needless to say, they don't appreciate his answer or his attitude. And quite frankly, I don't blame them. What arrogance!"

"I'm surprised to hear this! The managers I've spoken to seem to like James. But I'll look into it if you like."

"Yes. Do that. Still, to make sure there're no more complaints, I'm thinking about taking over the coaching project myself. Treblid is new here and obviously doesn't understand how we work here at MDL. I've told him several times, but he doesn't seem to listen. I can't have one of my people acting like the Lone Ranger. We should put him on a team-building program – would do him a world of good. The coaching project's too big for him."

There's a long silence.

"And another thing, Roger, your three-month performance appraisal of Treblid doesn't help the situation either!"

"What do you mean?"

"You missed some things. Your performance ratings were much too generous. What's he proven so far? Other than doing things his own way without going through the proper channels. Look at how he got the coaching idea going. Did he come to you or me first? No. He did it his own way. I can't accept that. Can we trust this man? I'm not at all convinced."

"Well..."

"Do you know why managers in this company call me before making decisions about transferring or promoting their own people? Aside from my being VP of Human Resources, it's because they trust my judgment. They see the way I manage my people and wish they could get the same respect from theirs. Besides, I practically have my Masters Degree in Psychology. I know how to motivate people. They know this, and that's why they seek my advice. Do you understand what I mean? So, for the next appraisal, for Pete's sake, be more realistic with your rating. He still has a lot to learn."

"But he's doing a terrific job in training. It's running very well and..."

"Roger, you're not listening to what I've been saying, so let me say it again. Treblid is doing what we pay him to do – nothing more. Don't make him look better than he is. Is this clear?"

"Maybe if..."

"I'll let him go a little further with the pilot project, then I'll remove him. Do you have any other questions?"

"No."

I don't bother stopping the tape as I stare at the machine in shock. That son of a bitch! How could he? I jump out of my chair, open the door and ask Rose to come into the office. "Rose, you have no idea where this tape came from?"

"None."

"Maybe it's Kitchell! They don't like each other much – maybe it's her way of getting back at Zaco. Then again, it might be Roger!" My mind races. I look at Rose. "Have you let anyone else listen to this?"

She shakes her head.

"Good." I point at the tape. "Rose, you're right; this is illegal, but coming from Zaco, it doesn't surprise me. He'll get what's coming to him soon enough. Confronting him with this now will send him into major denial and make everyone's life miserable. We need to think this through some more and come up with a way to keep the coaching project away from him and expose him for who he really is. Can we keep this to ourselves for now?"

Rose nods. "If I have to." And she walks out, shaking her head.

I look at my watch and realize that the technicians are going to be here in less than an hour. I've got to put this out of my mind for now and get ready for the meeting.

〜〜

This is a tough-looking bunch – 22 technicians, one half belonging to Ben Amber who are designated the test group and the other half to Don Brit, supervisor of the control group. They look like they would rather be somewhere else. I can see why some of the supervisors were concerned when they learned about the evaluation process.

I sense a lot of apprehension, so I begin slowly. "Good afternoon, everyone. I'm James Treblid, the Training Manager. You're here this afternoon to participate in a pilot project."

"Great! Another experiment!" yells someone from the back.

Ignoring the comment, I say "The project is to help your bosses become better coaches."

One guy shouts out "It's about time!" A burst of laughter follows.

"The first step is to evaluate how they're doing now. And yeah, it may be the first time that some of you actually get to rate your bosses' performance, but be careful. Sure you can dump all over them or blow sunshine up their rear-ends just to flatter their egos, but you won't be doing yourselves any favours. The purpose of the project is to make your department better – that means a better place to work so it becomes a better performing place. So if you're not honest with your feelings or perceptions about the situation in your department, everyone loses – the company, your boss and you. It's that simple."

The room is silent.

To lighten the mood, I add, "And for heaven's sake, don't put your name on the questionnaire!" Another burst of laughter erupts.

One of the mechanics yells out, "Can I put someone else's name instead?" Everyone cracks up again.

"No names from anyone. This is an individual and anonymous exercise. So give it an honest effort, please. When you're finished, leave the

139

questionnaires on the desk and you can leave afterwards. Any questions?"

"What about pencils?"

"Sure. I'll pass them around too."

~~

As I hand out the questionnaires, I notice Roger, my boss, standing at the door, one hand in his pocket and the other scratching his beard. I give him a signal that I'll be right over.

It's not easy to act innocent. "Hi, Roger! What's up?"

He sounds nervous. "James, I have to talk to you."

"Sure!" I say brightly.

We step outside where we won't be heard but where I can still keep an eye on the group.

"We've got a problem." He sounds serious.

"What kind of problem?"

"I'm getting complaints from managers that you're not providing the training they're asking for."

Without a trace of emotion, I ask, "What kind of training do you mean?"

"New products! They're complaining that you're not giving their people or their customers new product training on time!"

"Do you mean the Sales people or the Customer Service people?"

"Both!"

I sigh and nod my head.

"James, you've got to understand the pressure I'm under here. I'm getting it from all sides." He pauses for a moment before dropping a bomb. "Do you think we could postpone this coaching thing for awhile?"

I can't believe it. "What the hell are you talking about? Postpone it? Are you nuts?"

Not exactly the best thing I could've said.

Roger straightens; he's avoiding my eye. "Listen, I know this project is important to you, but we've got to take care of business first."

I try to control my anger. "Okay. I hear you. Roger, the guys and I have thought about this problem for some time now and I think we have a solution. Let me finish up here first then meet me in my office in 15 minutes. Okay?"

He shakes his head. "I'd like to, but I have another meeting in a few minutes."

"So when can I see you?"

"Not this week." He pauses and looks me straight in the eye. "Zaco will call you in a couple of days."

Now I can't hide my frustration. "Is he trying to take over the coaching project?"

He looks at me and finally nods. "James, all I can say is, be ready." He turns and walks away.

I go back into the classroom; the technicians are starting to file out. I pick up the questionnaires and return to my office.

What About You? _____

- How do office politics influence your organization's climate and performance?

_____

_____

_____

- List 3 of the most challenging people you've worked with during your career. Why were they challenging?

_____

_____

_____

- Do you like to be evaluated? Why?

_____

_____

_____

continued

- Do you think most people like to be evaluated?

  _____

  _____

  _____

- In your career, who would you have liked to have a chance to evaluate, but haven't? Why?

  _____

  _____

  _____

- How would your subordinates evaluate your Credibility, Desire to Coach, Skills and Capacity?

  _____

  _____

  _____

TEST YOURSELF and your SUPERVISOR

Answer each statement according to the following scale:
Almost never - 1   Sometimes - 2   Regularly - 3   Almost always - 4

53. In your work group, people have the opportunity to develop new skills.　　1　　2　　3　　4

54. In your work group, people are encouraged to do whatever it takes to satisfy a customer's needs.　　1　　2　　3　　4

55. As a manager, you have the time to follow the personal development of each one of your subordinates.　　1　　2　　3　　4

56. From your perspective, your superior has the time to follow your personal development.　　1　　2　　3　　4

57. As a manager, you have the information to properly manage the personal development of your subordinates.　　1　　2　　3　　4

58. From your perspective, your superior has the information to properly manage your personal development.　　1　　2　　3　　4

Chapter 10

The Analyses

Preview _____

James must manage the emotions and the reasons behind a poor evaluation. Following an in-depth review of the features of an effective coach, James must somehow find the courage and grace to present bad news sensitively. He must also find a way to get the supervisor to move past denial and begin to accept the information before change can occur.

"Come in, Ben." I get up to welcome him into the conference room.

Unlike the first time, his rugged hand feels damp. I can feel his uneasiness.

"How does it look?" he asks nervously.

This isn't the same confident man I met yesterday. He's obviously anxious to see how he scored on the survey, even if he believes the results were predictable.

"Let's take a look," I say, and head to the conference table. "I want to go over the results together, but first I'd like to review some of the basic definitions one more time. Okay?"

"Sure."

"Let's start with the four principal factors. The first one is 'credibility.' In the questionnaire you all filled out, there are five questions related to credibility. Here's the list of characteristics."

Respect: The esteem a subordinate has for a supervisor.

Dedication: A supervisor's demonstrated commitment to a cause; "the supervisor works harder than anyone else in the group."

Honesty: A supervisor's straightforwardness and adherence to the facts.

Role Model: The supervisor is an example of conduct for the subordinates.

Technical Competence: The supervisor has a thorough understanding of the technical issues.

Team-Focus / Strategy: Team oriented; that is, activities and decisions made by the supervisor are always in the best interest of the group, as opposed to an individual member of the group; in the end, the team plays, wins and loses as a group. Day-to-day decisions made by the supervisor are consistent with pre-set objectives and plans. All decisions are made with the same objective in mind: to hit a specific target (win an event or attain a specific level of competence). The greater the consistency, the greater the credibility.

Leadership: The state of effectively directing a group of individuals towards a specified goal.

Personal Values: Ethical – having high moral standards on the job.

I look at Ben and ask, "Any questions?"

He shakes his head.

"The second principal factor is 'desire to.' It's defined as 'the supervisor's willingness to undertake specific coaching tasks.'"

"I remember," Ben says.

"Good. Here's an example, Question #38, 'If necessary, is the coach willing to be firm?', or Question #17, 'willing to give individual attention'?"

"I'm sure we'll see some high and low scores here," says Ben a little bitterly.

"Here's the full list of characteristics we assessed."

Discipline: Correct or penalize for improper conduct.

Firmness: Be steadfast on proper conduct.

Individual Attention: Provide specific attention to each subordinate.

Flexibility: Respond to a changing situation.

Feedback / Evaluation: Assess and comment on an individual's performance.

Personal Development: Explore an employee's career track.

Relates to Others: Enjoy social interaction and is sensitive to other people's needs.

Ben reviews the list and grimaces at the thought of how he might be rated by his subordinates.

Before he can make any comments, I go on. "The third principal factor is 'skills'; that is, the ability to successfully complete an activity, alone and with others. As you can see, skills are divided into two distinct sub-groups: people skills and task skills. Take a few minutes to review both lists."

People Skills

Communication: Ability to deliver the information intended.

Teaching: Ability to instruct.

Listening: Ability to receive the information intended.

Interpersonal Relationships: Ability to establish and maintain rapport with all the members of a group.

Consultative: Ability to consult with members of a group before making a decision.

Contingent Reinforcement: Ability to provide effective feedback following a specific outcome.

Task skills

Setting Objectives: Ability to identify challenging and reasonable individual and group goals.

Organization / Anticipation: Ability to prioritize and co-ordinate activities for the purpose of attaining a specific goal.

Preparation: Ability to gather data beforehand and understand pertinent information.

Practice / Perfection: Ability to plan and execute effective training sessions.

Delegation: Ability to strategically spread the workload among subordinates.

Follow-up: Ability to observe and intervene in post-training results.

"Any questions?"

"Not really."

"You know, Ben, all these characteristics are equally important. Some of the people I interviewed put a lot of emphasis on four of them: 'Teaching,' 'Practice,' 'Non-verbal Communication' and 'Delegation.' Let's take a closer look at their meanings and uses."

"'Teaching' underscores the point that an effective coach should be constantly alert to opportunities for transferring knowledge or for instructing a subordinate on performance matters. For example, if an employee is having a problem with a specific process, the coach will intervene by first evaluating the situation and then instructing the right approach in a clear and positive manner."

"'Practice' is a concept that's more widely used in sports than in business. The interesting aspect, however, is that in management as in sport, the greater the quantity and quality of practice, the better the skill is executed in the field. Execution of the skill becomes automatic and the doubt that often creeps into the user's consciousness is removed. The more a skill is practiced, the greater self-confidence a user acquires in applying it in a real situation. Just think of the military and the importance it places on training exercises. They virtually never stop training, until maneuvers are executed almost unconsciously and flawlessly."

"Yeah, but how does that apply to us?" asks Ben.

"The same way it applies to athletes, doctors, scientists, bankers, airline pilots, electricians and plumbers. In fact, it applies to everyone who faces challenging situations in their jobs that could require swift and precise diagnosis, decisions and actions – every time. For us, it means reacting correctly to business situations, whether it's product, process, people or competitor driven. Our sales people, machine technicians and managers must all have an automatic reflex when faced with urgent and not necessarily important customer issues. If we panic, we lose our focus. And that's one step away from losing our cool."

"I'm not saying we need to practice for every possible situation, but rather we should be well schooled in the fundamentals which might apply to most situations. For example, our sales people should have an almost automatic response to a customer who raises an objection about our products or services. Like when a customer says, 'I can't buy from you because you're too expensive.' The sales rep should have had enough practice to address and overcome the objection in a professional and maybe even casual manner. Or how about when a customer comes in the shops, ranting and raving about his machine breakdown. How do we react? And more importantly, what do we do? Or how about when an employee says to you, without thinking first, 'you're nuts! I'm not taking that job order.' What's your immediate reaction? What do you say? Because the very next words out of your mouth will set the tone and determine the probability for a quick and effective resolution to the immediate problem and establish the precedent for the future. And you know as well as I do that one moment can make the difference between a happy relationship and a destructive one."

"I guess so," says Ben.

"The other skill that requires some explanation is 'Delegation.' It's another 'Task Skill' that seems underrated in everyday business life. The people I interviewed in the research are unequivocal on this point – the ability to delegate tasks and responsibilities to subordinates is among the most important characteristics of successful coaches. Typically, because of the range of responsibilities and subsequent tasks a coach undertakes, it's not unusual for the coach to be simply overwhelmed by the events. Unless he shares or delegates the workload, failure to reach the goals is imminent. Interesting, isn't it?"

"That's fine for big bosses who have secretaries, but who the hell am I supposed to delegate to? My boss?"

"Good question. For now, let's just say you might be right. Let's keep going."

"One of the coaches I interviewed revealed three critical sub-skills or personality attributes that we don't hear about very often. I mention them here for two reasons. First, because of the respect I have for the coach who said it; and second, it just makes a lot of sense. I believe they should be part of the required skill sets for effective coaching. At any rate, the pilot project will confirm if these attributes are important or not."

"The first one is 'Anticipation' – the ability to look ahead and avoid surprises. This sub-skill is related to 'organization' skills because it represents an ability to plan and forecast probable events that could negatively impact on performance. A strong sense of anticipation minimizes potential disasters and maximizes favourable opportunities. Like the coach says, 'even if you can't stop the storm from coming, you can prepare yourself to minimize the property damage.'"

"An important attribute associated with successful coaches is their need for 'Perfection.' Perfection is associated with a coach's extreme desire to practice perfectly so that in the field a skill is performed automatically and flawlessly. This emphasizes the need for greater quantity and quality of training sessions – especially practical application exercises where an individual is required to execute a learned skill repeatedly. The result is a skill that's executed competently every time."

"Finally, the 'Look' is the last sub-skill emphasized. It's another effective method of communication. The supervisor communicates his viewpoint with his eyes only. This sub-skill is especially effective in situations relating to issues that don't require any further explanation. For example, improper conduct by a subordinate within a group setting might require only a 'look' by the supervisor. In these situations, it is expected that everyone, especially the targeted subordinate, readily understand the supervisor's silent message; that is, 'that conduct is inappropriate.' This type of feedback is very effective when there's no need for a long and verbose reprimand. A 'look' by the coach is also effective and sufficient in very positive situations where an individual meets and exceeds expectations on an on-going basis. Words of praise and appreciation can be substituted with a 'look' or other non-verbal gestures like a handshake or a thumbs-up."

"The fourth and final principal factor, 'Capacity,' is defined as 'the availability and deployment of resources.' It's a relatively new management term that represents 'freedom of constraints' – constraints that usually bind and confine an organization and its people from acting in a given situation. Some call it excess capacity, or 'having a little more resource than what is exactly required.' Here's the list."

Time: An irrecoverable resource.

Support: The assistance of superiors, colleagues and subordinates.

Financial Resources: A financial resource/critical element of the reward system.

Information: A strategic input for decision making.

Equipment: A material resource.

Talent: A pool of human resources.

"Each one of these attributes is essential to a successful coaching program. Without them, the program fails. How often do we hear: 'I don't have the time, money or equipment to do the job right?' Or 'I'm not getting the support from above?' Or 'If people don't tell me what's going on, how can I instruct my people?' Clearly, the quantity and quality of resources available and deployed in organizations are core elements of effective coaching programs."

"'Space' is not part of the 'capacity' list, yet it warrants investigation because of its obvious impact on performance. It's described as the physical distance between a player and his coach. In sport, the physical closeness during an event is critical. The coach provides on-the-job direction and feedback. It's traditional and accepted as part of the event. In a management setting, post-training follow-up could benefit from a similar environment in which supervisors spend more time in closer proximity with their subordinates."

I pause to let the information sink in and ask: "You okay so far?"

He replies, "I'm fine, keep going."

"Okay then. Let's look at how you did."

I put up the scores on the overhead projector and look back at Ben.

He's totally concentrated on the scores and the results. Before I can say anything, he puts his face in his hands and lets out a loud sigh. "Jesus, it's worse than I thought." He leans back in his chair and asks, "What the hell am I supposed to do now?"

I start gently. "First, let's take a look at how the information is organized so that you can understand how the results were attained. Then we'll analyze what they mean. And finally, we'll decide together what you might want to do next."

"Let's start with what the columns represent. The first column identifies the questions 1 to 45. The second column denotes the factor or

DEPARTMENT: General Service
DATE: April
GROUP: Customer Service
SUPERVISOR: Ben Amber
MANAGER/BOSS: George Pike

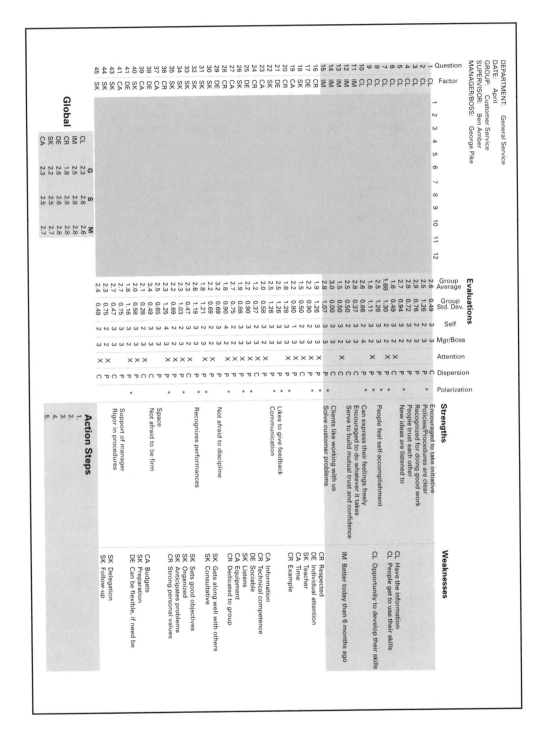

Evaluations

Question	Factor	Group Average	Group Std. Dev.	Self	Mgr/Boss	Attention	Dispersion	Polarization
1	CL	2.6	0.49	3	3		C	
2	CL	2.5	1.26	3	3		P	
3	CL	2.9	0.76	3	3		C	
4	CL	2.8	0.72	2	3		C	
5	CL	2.7	0.94	3	3	×	C	*
6	CL	1.6	0.49	3	3		C	
7	CL	1.68	1.30	2	2	× ×	C	*
8	CL	2.5	1.26	3	3		C	
9	CL	1.6	1.11	2	4	×	C	*
10	CL	2.6	0.86	3	3		C	
11	IM	2.8	0.37	3	3		C	
12	IM	2.5	0.50	2	3	× × × ×	C	* * * *
13	IM	2.5	0.50	3	3		C	
14	IM	1.5	0.50	3	3		C	
15	IM	3.0	0.00	2	2	×	C	
16	CR	2.8	1.07	3	3		C	
17	DE	1.9	1.26	2	3	× × × ×	P	* * *
18	SK	2.2	0.90	2	3		P	
19	CA	1.5	0.50	2	3		C	
20	CR	2.2	0.80	1	3		P	
21	DE	1.8	1.28	3	2	×	P	*
22	SK	2.2	1.26	3	3	× × × × × ×	P	* *
23	CA	2.5	1.26	3	3		P	
24	CR	2.0	0.58	2	3		P	
25	DE	1.2	0.37	3	3		C	
26	SK	1.9	0.90	3	3	× ×	P	* *
27	CA	2.2	0.86	3	3		C	
28	CR	2.7	0.75	4	2		C	
29	DE	1.8	0.90	2	3		C	
30	SK	3.2	0.90	2	2	× ×	C	*
31	SK	1.8	0.69	2	2		C	
32	SK	2.2	0.69	2	3		P	
33	SK	1.8	1.21	4	3		P	
34	SK	2.3	0.47	2	3		C	
35	SK	2.3	1.19	3	3		P	
36	CR	2.5	1.03	3	3	× ×	P	*
37	CA	2.3	0.69	3	3		C	
38	DE	3.4	0.65	2	2	× ×	P	
39	CA	2.5	0.49	3	3		C	
40	CA	2.0	1.25	3	3		C	
41	DE	1.8	0.58	2	3		C	
42	CA	2.0	0.28	3	3		C	
43	SK	2.7	1.16	3	3	× ×	P	*
44	SK	2.3	0.47	3	3		C	
45	SK	2.4	0.75	2	3		P	

Strengths

- Solve customer problems
- Clients like working with us
- Serve to build mutual trust and confidence
- Encouraged to do whatever it takes
- Can express their feelings freely
- People feel self-accomplishment
- New ideas are listened to
- People trust each other
- Recognized for doing good work
- Policies/Procedures are clear
- Encouraged to take initiative
- Communication
- Likes to give feedback
- Not afraid to discipline
- Recognizes performances
- Not afraid to be firm
- Space
- Support of manager
- Rigor in procedures

Weaknesses

- IM Better today than 6 months ago
- CL Opportunity to develop their skills
- CL People get to use their skills
- CL Have the information
- CA Information
- CR Technical competence
- DE Sociable
- SK Listens
- CA Equipment
- CR Dedicated to group
- CR Respected
- DE Individual attention
- SK Teacher
- CA Time
- CR Example
- SK Gets along well with others
- SK Consultative
- SK Sets good objectives
- SK Organized
- SK Anticipates problems
- CR Strong personal values
- CA Budgets
- SK Preparation
- DE Can be flexible, if need be
- SK Delegation
- SK Follow-up

Global

	G	S	M
CL	2.3	2.6	2.6
IM	2.5	2.6	2.8
CR	1.8	2.8	2.8
DE	2.6	2.6	2.8
SK	2.2	2.5	2.7
CA	2.3	2.5	2.7

Action Steps

1.
2.
3.
4.
5.

performance indicator the question relates to. For example, CL is for the department's 'climate'; IM is for the 'image' projected by the department; CR stands for 'credibility'; DE stands for 'desire to coach'; SK stands for 'skills'; and finally, CA stands for 'capacity.' The next 12 columns headed with numbers 1 to 12 are the hidden scores given by your employees; this is to preserve individual confidentiality and deter the manager from guessing which employee scored him low – especially in groups with only a handful of subordinates. The column 'Group Average' is the sum of the scores for each question divided by the number of respondents. The next column 'Group STD. DEV.' represents the variance in the group score. The next two columns are the scores you gave yourself and your boss's respectively. In the 'Attention' column, an 'X' appears if the 'Group Average' is less than '2.5' – this is a signal that an opportunity for improvement exists. An 'X' also appears if the average of your score and that of your boss is less than '2.5.' In the next column, 'Dispersion,' the letter 'C' means that the scores are concentrated or unanimous; the letter 'P' means they're more spread out. In the next column, 'Polarization,' an asterisk means that there's a significant split in the group scores. The last two columns present the strengths and areas of improvement for the supervisor."

"Finally, at the bottom, there are two boxes, 'Global' and 'Action Steps.' In the first is a summary of the scores – it'll give us a general picture of your profile; in the other you'll find the steps to be taken to overcome the weaknesses."

I look up at Amber and he looks totally dejected, but I continue.

"The first 15 questions, shaded in gray, relate to 'Climate' and 'Image.' Even though the coach has an impact on these areas, it's also heavily influenced by the rest of the organization and therefore requires the intervention of the boss as well. Questions 16 to 45 deal with you, the supervisor."

For the next 30 minutes, I go over the results, line by line.

Ben is clearly very upset.

Before discussing the 'Global' and 'Action Steps,' I pause. "Ben I can only imagine how you feel, but in order to get over the sting of these scores you should make a decision here. You can either take all of this and throw it out the window, or decide that you're going to try to make some changes." I let him think about it for a moment.

He looks at me gravely. "James, this is bad. I can understand some of the scores; I know there are areas I need to improve – skills like 'teaching,' 'anticipating problems' and 'delegation' have never been my strong points. But what really hurts are the scores I got for 'credibility' – I can't believe people doubt my values or dedication to the group. That really hurts!"

I feel for him. "There's a saying: 'bad news doesn't get better with age.' This is why you need to decide if you're going to forget about it or do something. And I think it's better you make the call here and now, without waiting."

He's angry and I understand why. "Those bastards!"

After a few minutes of silence, he looks at me. I can tell it hurts to say it, but he does: "Okay. Let's do something."

"Good!" Without any further comment I move into the action steps. "Overall, the areas that need to be addressed are the department's climate, your credibility, your capacity to develop your people and finally your skills to be an effective coach."

I go on to explain the need for him to discuss with his boss the areas that are negatively affecting the department's climate the most – especially with regards to information and skill use. I suspect it has something to do with training: "Why do you think theses scores are so low?"

"We're always waiting for training on new machines," he snaps.

I nod. "Yeah. I know all about it. I'll be presenting a plan to Lester Zaco in a few days. If he goes for it, it'll help fix the situation."

"Good."

I go on to explain to him the need for a captain to help him temporarily with his credibility. He's skeptical at first but eventually buys into the idea and selects two people from his department as possible candidates – one for the old guys and one for the new ones. Finally, I suggest a personalized training program to give him the skills to teach adults, organize and anticipate his work environment, improve interpersonal relationships, and sell and negotiate for more 'capacity.'

Ben seems to like the action steps. "I don't know if all this is going to work, but I'm ready to give it my best shot."

"That's all I can ask for," I say, pleased.

We talk about scheduling the training and the monthly follow-ups to review his progress. I mention the tests and cases that'll be used to check his retention of the skills he'll learn.

By the end of our meeting, he seems more relaxed. In fact, he leaves with a smile.

≈

I gather my notes and walk back to my office. Charles Renacks is talking to Rose.

"Hi, Charles," I say with little enthusiasm.

"James!" he sings out. "Just the person I wanted to see!" He follows me into my office and closes the door. "I came by to find out when you were going to meet with me to discuss my results?"

I'm surprised but I try to be tactful. "Charles, only the managers of the test groups are put through the coaching program at this time. Because you're part of the control group, your results will be disclosed after a second survey is done in six months. For now only Dan Wetomy, your Regional Sales Manager, is put through the process, remember?"

He looks crestfallen. "Oh!" Then: "Well, how did Dan do on the evaluation?"

"He told me he'd prefer to keep the results confidential for now and he'd talk to you about it later. All I can say is that we agreed to some skills training which would not take him out of the field for more than three days."

Charles seems offended. "Shouldn't I know about this?"

"He should let you know about the training, yes. As for the entire profile, well, that's up to him. Remember, we talked about this at our meeting and all agreed that it was okay if the manager wanted to keep the results to himself."

"Yeah, yeah – I remember."

Then, out of the blue, he blurts out: "James, I understand that Lester Zaco might be taking over the project."

I give him a blank look.

"Must be upsetting for you," he says a little smugly.

Unable to contain my irritation, I fire back, "Where'd you hear that?'

His grin is maddening. "Oops! I thought you knew."

"Listen, Charles. I know you and Zaco are pretty tight. I also know that some of the managers are complaining to him about the Training department not delivering the training they want. You wouldn't be one of them, would you?"

"James, it's no secret that you guys aren't doing the job you're supposed to be doing," he says icily.

"What are you trying to say?"

"If I were you, I'd get my house in order before pushing this coaching project of yours any further."

"Thanks. I'll look into it." I turn my back on him, but not before I see him smirk on his way out.

What About You? _____

- Think of a situation where you received bad news. How did you feel? How did you react?

  _____

  _____

  _____

- Think of a situation where you delivered bad news. How did you feel? How did you react?

  _____

  _____

  _____

- How do you think your superior and your subordinates would evaluate your coaching style?

  _____

  _____

  _____

TEST YOURSELF and your SUPERVISOR

Answer each statement according to the following scale:
Almost never - 1   Sometimes - 2   Regularly - 3   Almost always - 4

59. As a manager, you want to give individual attention to each subordinate in your work group.   1   2   3   4

60. Your superior wants to give individual attention to you.   1   2   3   4

61. As a manager, you like giving feedback.   1   2   3   4

62. From your perspective, your superior likes to give feedback.   1   2   3   4

63. As a manager, you're not afraid of being firm with the group, if required.   1   2   3   4

64. From your perspective, your superior is not afraid of being firm with the group, if required.   1   2   3   4

Chapter 11

The Challenges

Preview

James faces losing the coaching project. With the help of
Charlene and some basic physics, James presents a strategy to
Zaco that he hopes will solve the productivity problems and stop
the complaints from internal customers. It turns into a classic
"selling" and "negotiation" session.

"What's wrong?" Charlene asks as I walk in the door.

"The damn politics in that place are killing me!"

"What happened?"

I take off my coat and move to the living room. Charlene hands me a glass of wine and I begin explaining the events of the day – the tape recording, Roger's warning and Renacks's intimidation.

"Wow! Your coaching project is really hitting a nerve with some people!"

I nod.

"Let's have dinner and talk about it during our walk later. In the meantime, I've got some great news for you!"

"You do?"

She's all smiles. "I was talking to a publisher friend of mine and we got on the subject of your coaching model. Well, she's very interested in it. So much so that she wants you to meet her to see if you'd be willing to publish it!"

I can hardly believe my ears. "What? Are you kidding me?'

"Nope," she says, laughing. "She thinks you're really on to something and wants to explore it with you! I said you'd call her. Is that okay?"

"That's outstanding! What's her name?"

"Mandy Sotrap."

"Terrific! Give me her number and I'll call her!" I rush over to give her a big hug.

All the aggression and anger I'd bottled up seems to melt away.

〜〜〜

The fresh night air feels good, as it always does. With renewed energy, I begin telling Charlene all about my day. "I'm meeting with Zaco later this week. It seems he's going to pull me off of the pilot project – and I'm not sure I can stop him."

"What do you think's causing all this commotion?"

"The way I see it, there're two things going on. One, Zaco wants control of the coaching program – he sees it as big-time feather in his cap and doesn't want someone else taking the credit for it. The other thing is the logjam in the Training department – especially for new product training. We're getting swamped with requests from our Sales and Customer Service groups and we can't deliver. So they're complaining to Roger and Zaco about it. My guess is that now that the managers have been evaluated, Zaco sees an opportunity to get control of the information and somehow use it to his advantage."

"Hmm… That's tough. I know coaching's your baby and you don't want to let it go, but you have to survive first. And that means making sure your operations are running smoothly; otherwise you're giving them a reason for taking it away."

I try not to sound defensive. "How am I supposed to do that if I don't have the right information or the manpower?"

She takes my hand. "Zaco might be a scheming creep but he's not stupid – he knows how to keep his boss happy. I'm not sure why, but I have a feeling that you know the answer. It's there somewhere in the back of your mind. If you approach the situation as a 'capacity' problem first, what would you do?" Before I can reply, she adds, "Take a lesson from your model, honey: before you meet Zaco, you need to have your case ready and to be prepared to sell and negotiate."

She didn't have to say anything else. It's time to practice what I've been preaching. The first thing I need to do is meet with Tom Wunkler and then the trainers to explain my plan for increasing the department's ability to deliver training – that is, get more capacity. Without their support, my plan won't fly. The next thing is to carefully prepare the case I'll present to Zaco. There are two objectives: one, to get agreement on the plan for increasing the department's output; and two, to retain my control of the coaching project. If I can keep his attention long enough on the issue of output and get him to discover what I discovered, it seems to me he'll be willing to let me continue with the pilot project. I just have to remain calm, not get emotional. If I can weather the first couple of minutes, make it through his usual outbursts, I'll be okay. After that it's a matter of selling and negotiating.

〜〜

As usual, Zaco's secretary, Betty, is totally concentrated with something on her computer screen. She doesn't see me arrive and I startle her with my "Good Morning." She recovers quickly and tells me to walk right into her boss's office.

I knock on the door before opening it. To my surprise, I'm face to face with Roger! As I walk in, he closes the door behind me. There's no coffee this time and I sense the tension in the air. I sit down in one of the wingback chairs, once again sinking below Zaco's eye level. I don't react.

Zaco waits for me to settle before leaning in. "James, we need to address your attitude. We've been receiving very negative comments from line managers and customers about your department's performance. So I've decided it's time for a change."

I'm thinking to myself – James, don't get emotional here, stay rational, stay with your plan.

"Oh?" My tone's casual. "What do you mean?"

He raises his voice a little. "It bothers me to know that you're spending so much time on coaching and so little on what we pay you to do – and that's running the Training department! We've already warned you about this once!"

"Who is 'we'?" It's a flippant comeback, verging on insubordination, and I know it, but it slips out before I can help it.

He's clearly annoyed. "That's exactly what your problem is, Treblid! You don't listen! Who the hell cares who 'we' is? I'm telling you – this is your problem. And it can't continue!"

I take a deep breath, look at Roger and then back at Zaco. "Okay, I agree. The department is having problems, serious problems with delivery. But I have a plan. Can I talk to you about it?"

Zaco looks at Roger and back at me. "Plan? What plan?" I've thrown him off course, at least momentarily.

I immediately get up and walk over to the flip chart next to his desk. With a felt pen I draw what looks like a four-inch pipe entering a two-inch pipe and back again into a four-inch pipe.

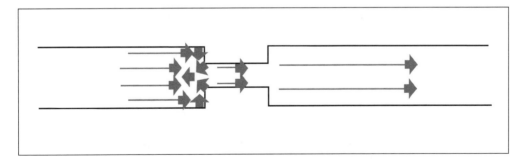

I look up at Zaco. "This is our system." Before they can react, I continue. "Think of these pipes as the conduits for information into our company. The big pipe on the left is carrying the information provided by the manufacturer, which we need to know to effectively sell and service our machines. The little pipe in the middle is the Training department through which all the information now goes through. The big pipe on the right is the information that's being used by our reps, their customers and, of course, our own technicians."

Neither of them says anything, so I go on. "The arrows indicate the volume of information flowing through the system. As the information approaches the little pipe – the Training department – you can see by the arrows that the flow of information gets interrupted – some of it backs up and some gets compressed to fit into the little pipe. The additional pressure in the small pipe doesn't mean more volume. In fact, the result is that once the information reaches the pipe on the right, the pressure drops and the volume remains the same – meaning that the pipe is only part full."

"What you're saying," Roger interjects, "is that the Training department doesn't have the capacity to handle all the volume of information that needs to be passed on to our people, right?"

"Right. Our capacity is determined by the number of trainers and the time available."

Zaco jumps in. "Are you saying you need more damn trainers?"

"Not necessarily. Let me explain why. The problem is one of capacity, that's true. But to simply increase the number of trainers might not be the most efficient solution. First, the information doesn't arrive in a nice even flow – it fluctuates a lot. Just think about how unpredictable the launch of new products is. Some months there's nothing and others we could get hit with four new machines! Everyone scrambles for the new information and the pressure on the Training department is incredible. But our output can't be greater than what our capacity will allow – no matter how much pressure is put into the department."

"That makes sense!" Roger says, avoiding Zaco's glare.

"Second, there are other times when the volume of information wouldn't even fill the little pipe in the diagram. So to simply increase the number of trainers would be a poor use of resources."

Zaco nods reluctantly.

I continue, "There's a whole science behind managing fluctuations and bottlenecks. If we understand its underpinnings, we'll find the solution to our problem." I pause for a moment. "Can I continue?"

They both nod.

"The fundamental premise is that the maximum output of a closed system is equal to the output of its tightest bottleneck. What this means is that, in a system where there're many different pipe sizes, the final output will not exceed the maximum output of its smallest pipe. In the diagram above, the output of the pipe on the right will never exceed the output of the middle pipe – the bottleneck."

"So why have such a big pipe on the right?"

"Good question!" I reply. "It seems like a waste, doesn't it? All that capacity sitting there, never being used. Another way of looking at it, though, is that the 'slack' or extra capacity in this pipe has no effect on the final output. So to spend money to make it smaller might be a bigger waste of resources. The key to maximizing output is to successfully manage the bottlenecks."

"How do we do that?" asks Roger.

"There are two ways. One, increase the capacity of the bottleneck, or two, improve the quality of the material flowing through it."

"I don't understand," Zaco grumbles.

"Let's take a look at what happens in the Training department – the little pipe in the middle. First, we often find out about new products just before they arrive in the yard. Second, our trainers have to go to the manufacturer and learn about the machines. Third, the trainer has to design a training program for our people. Fourth, the trainer has to deliver the program to all Sales and Service personnel, here and at our branch offices. All these activities are done in this little pipe. Can you imagine how much of our capacity is used up for things other than delivering training?"

They both nod again. I think they're getting the picture.

"What I'm saying is that if we could do any of these four steps more efficiently, we could increase our capacity; or, putting it another way, have more time to deliver training. For example, if we could get some inside information from the manufacturer about new products much sooner than we do now, our trainers could prepare their training courses during slack times in the Training department. This would reduce the preparation time that's now needed during periods of high demand – when the little pipe is full – when we're really a bottleneck and all the capacity should be used for delivering training."

"That's a good point," says Zaco.

"And there's something else we could do," I say, pretending to hesitate. "But it's going to require a strong leader to champion it."

"Oh? What's that?" asks Zaco. He's interested.

"Remember the discussion we had about the optimal group size for training?"

"Yeah."

"Well, one way to improve the quality of the information in the bottleneck is to offer richer or higher-grade course content."

"What do you mean?"

"Let's go back to the diagram. If, for example, we added another pipe that goes directly from one big pipe to the other and bypasses the bottleneck all together, what do you think would happen?"

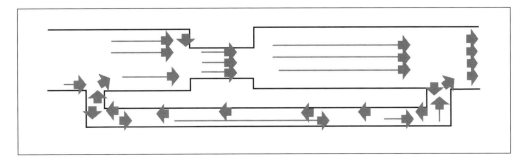

"The information goes directly from the manufacturer to the employees," Roger says. "But how do we do that?"

Before I can answer, Zaco breaks in. "A shift in our learning culture!" Now he's sounding downright enthusiastic. "James, you're talking about getting our employees to learn on their own. That'll reduce the pressure on the Training department." He pauses for a moment. "Brilliant! I see it now. Get the employees to learn some product content on their own, before and after the training classes. Trainers will offer a higher-grade of information because the technicians will come to class with a pre-determined amount of knowledge. We could focus on the critical information instead of starting from scratch like we do now. This would cut down on class time and translate into more training classes, the result being a much greater training output."

I grin. "It'll also require some post-training follow-up by the managers."

Zaco beams. "You're absolutely right! And I know I can sell this to the President!"

"Then it's okay that I continue with the pilot project?"

Zaco catches himself, takes a deep breath and smiles easily.

"No, it's not."

I feel numb. I want to say something, but I can't.

Zaco doesn't seem to notice. "What you've presented here is fine for the long term, but what about tomorrow and next week? What are you going to do about that?"

I pull myself together. "In the short term we could increase our output by bringing in an outside resource to expand our capacity."

Zaco grimaces. "You mean hire another trainer, don't you?"

"Not quite. Don't hire – borrow."

"What do you mean?" asks Roger.

"I mean we borrow an experienced technician from George Pike's crew – someone with training experience who's respected by his peers. I know he's got a few because my trainers suggested a couple of names yesterday."

Roger: "How would it work?"

"While our trainers focus on new products, the technician/trainer would deliver some of our existing courses that are currently in great demand – like the two-day "Diagnostic for Electronic Engines" course. We're swamped with requests; it's at least a three-month wait and people are screaming. So to have a technician/trainer deliver four or five of these courses in a row would relieve a lot of pressure. He'd be back in his old department in a couple of weeks. Now, if we had a couple of these technicians/trainers on temporary assignment with us, the training output would increase substantially."

Roger laughs. "I'm surprised George agreed to that!"

"He hasn't yet." I reply. "I haven't told him. I was hoping you or Mr. Zaco could persuade him to do it. He'd listen to you guys."

Zaco's flattered. "Yes, but what would we say to him?"

I pause for a moment, as if to collect my thoughts. "I'd start by telling him that we don't expect his department to do it for nothing. We'd cover his technician's wages and benefits for the time he's with us. Second, whatever revenue we generate from outside customer training during the same period, we'd share with his department, say, 30%. The other big benefit for George is that his other technicians would be trained immediately, which means more people to do service jobs and in turn that means more revenues for his department overall. If I know George, he'll like that a lot!"

"Maybe. What happens if he still objects?" asks Roger.

"Then you'll have to negotiate with him."

"Negotiate what?" asks Zaco.

"In return for the use of his men, you could offer the service of our trainers to do some overtime work or special duties during the slower training periods. I know some of the guys wouldn't mind the extra money."

Roger begins to take notes – a good sign.

"What else?" Zaco asks.

"Another thing would be to offer a greater percentage of external training revenues, from 30 to, say, 50%, or ask him what he wants and split the difference if that's what's holding up the agreement. And if that doesn't work, give him whatever he wants. In the end, we'll deliver the training and everyone will be happy – no more complaints."

Zaco asks, "How soon could you have a technician ready to train?"

"I'd say within three weeks."

Zaco nods his head in agreement and says, "I'll speak to George."

I jump in. "The pilot project?"

Still nodding, he replies, "Okay. Go ahead with your plans, but keep me posted on developments."

"I will." Smiling at both of them, I walk out of the office.

What About You? _____

- Identify 3 specific bottlenecks in your organization. What are the consequences? Are you a bottleneck?

  _____

  _____

  _____

  _____

  _____

- What is being done to relieve the back-pressure?

  _____

  _____

  _____

- What would you do to improve the effectiveness and efficiency of the organization?

  _____

  _____

  _____

  _____

  _____

  _____

TEST YOURSELF and your SUPERVISOR

Answer each statement according to the following scale:
Almost never - 1   Sometimes - 2   Regularly - 3   Almost always - 4

65. As a manager, you have the equipment to properly manage the development of each person in your work group.   1   2   3   4

66. From your perspective, your superior has the equipment to properly manage your development.   1   2   3   4

67. As a manager, you have the financial resources to adequately manage the development of your people.   1   2   3   4

68. From your perspective, your superior has the financial resources to adequately manage your development.   1   2   3   4

69. Your team (subordinates) has more talent than what is actually required to do the work.   1   2   3   4

70. From your perspective, your superior's team (subordinates) has more talent than what is actually required to do the work.   1   2   3   4

Chapter 12

The Results

Preview

James learns of the results of the pilot project and the impact on some of the people involved. In presenting the findings to the Executive Committee, James is surprised by an unexpected set of events that will profoundly affect his future at MDL.

September is a beautiful time of year. The trees in the neighbour-hood are beginning to show signs of crimson and gold. Fall is on its way.

The kids go back to school today, so I need to pay closer attention to the action on the street. I recognize most of the kids from last year and notice a few new faces. I see Max and Ty standing with a group of friends. I honk my horn and give them a wave. The first day of school is always exciting – a big day for everybody.

This is a big day for me too. I start off by meeting George Pike and his boss Norma Kitchell at 9:30, followed by the Executive Committee at 2:00 and finally, Lester Zaco. The meetings all have one thing in common – coaching, the results of the pilot project and its consequences for the organ-ization.

The last six months has been an exciting period for the Training department. Trainers are happy because they understand the goal and their individual contribution to reaching it. They have confidence in their manag-er and this is in no small part due to Tom Wunkler's role as captain.

The open cooperation received from the Sales and CS groups has also contributed to making it a fun environment to work in. We now have a direct link with the New Product Development Division at the manufactur-er. This gives us a six-month lead time to prepare training programs for new product launches. The results have been tremendous – the most recent launch was managed with minimum backlog for training. Even our outside customers are happy. This couldn't have happened if we hadn't added two part-time technicians/trainers to deliver internal training programs.

As I walk into the department, the trainers are milling about. Rose is laughing with Tom and Larry. It's nice to see everyone so happy. I open the door to my office, turn on the lights and it hits me! There's confetti, stream-ers, balloons, followed by a rousing, off-key chorus of *"Happy Birthday to you!"* Everyone applauds and approaches one by one to offer me best wish-es.

Frank and Larry surprise me the most; it's very touching, actually. In front of everybody Larry says, "James, we underestimated you. In less than a year you've turned this department around. For someone who didn't know the industry or the inner politics of MDL, you've managed to amaze and impress us all. Thanks and Happy Birthday."

I grin. "Thanks for the kind wishes. But give yourself some credit! I'm also amazed at how well you rose to the challenge of reaching these new goals. In the last six months we've increased our output by 30%. You took on new roles and brought about the necessary changes to make the department an efficient and effective unit. Congratulations."

They all applaud.

"There'll be more changes to come," I add. "And I think you're going to like them!"

〜〜

I arrive at Norma Kitchell's office and George is already there, waiting outside. To my surprise, so is Ben Amber, George's employee and participant in the pilot project. Before I can say anything, Kitchell walks out of her office and invites us all to come in.

I can't help but notice that most of the CS hierarchy is here – the Vice President, the Service Manager and the foreman. It strikes me for the first time that Norma Kitchell, George Pike and Ben Amber are cut from the same cloth. They're all honest, hardworking, customer-focused and profit-driven. They're also very sensitive about anyone in Corporate meddling in their affairs – especially Human Resources. 'Personnel' is okay, but not HR. Operations people view Personnel people as administrative support in wage & benefit administration, labour relations and government regulations. Their role is to execute and sometimes counsel, but never to decide unilaterally.

What scares the hell out of Operations people like these is the other side of HR – Organizational Development. This is the side where HR sits at the same table as they do with Finance and Marketing and participates in planning corporate strategies and tactics. From that point of view, they're often "the enemy."

Then there's the employee development side of HR. It lies somewhere between Personnel Administration and Organizational Development. For most, it means training – an important activity, performed by specialists, as long as it doesn't interfere with the business.

Kitchell begins unceremoniously. "James, I know you're presenting the results of the coaching project to the Executive today. I don't know what you're going to say or recommend, but I wanted to meet all of you beforehand.

"First, some of you will recall that when this pilot project was first proposed, I was opposed to it. In fact, extremely opposed. Remember, James?"

I nod.

Kitchell continues. "But here we are six months later, and I'm not

173

sure what to feel. I know that evaluations were done, training was given, and some good and bad results are on the board. George, you've got Ben's department exceeding plan and Britt's below; Ben, you're walking around with a smile I haven't seen in years; and James is a middle manager who's only been here for 10 months and has already had more contact with the Executive than most GMs. Can someone tell me what's going on?"

We all kind of smile. George says, "Norma, things are certainly different since Jimmy Boy arrived on the scene. We did some wheeling and dealing at first, but in the end our boys are getting more training than ever. The kicker though, is that they want more, and so do the foremen. Things are okay for now, but down the road, I don't have a clue how we're going to be able to handle it all. As far as the department's performance goes, well, Ben's done a great job – especially in the last quarter. We're doing more work with less overtime. Is it the coaching? I'm not sure. But one thing I'm certain about is that internal communication is a whole lot better!"

Kitchell looks at Ben. "What about you? What do you have to say?"

Ben is still smiling. "It's been an interesting ride. Six months ago I was feeling pretty low – I was new in the department, technicians were trying to transfer out, our P/L wasn't too good, and the poor rating I got on the first coaching evaluation was a real kick in the teeth. As time went on, though, I found the situation getting better. I put a couple of captains in place and got some real good training – especially in dealing with some of the old guys in the department. And the one on managing bottlenecks was a real eye opener. I also spend more time on the shop floor with the technicians. I'm not only surprised with how much I'm learning, but also how much I'm teaching, with very few words. Last week, James showed me the results of the second coaching evaluation. It's funny, but I wasn't surprised by the results."

Kitchell frowns. "Well, James, it's your turn."

"Look. Coaching isn't magic – it's common sense sprinkled with skills. My model exposes the common sense more than most other models. And if a manager is motivated, applying the model is easy and rewarding – for both the manager and the organization. One of the key requirements for an established company to adapt to change, especially in this era of super-quick turnover in technology and enormous amounts of available information, is its ability to communicate the right amount to the right people at the right time. And as far as I'm concerned, this is the manager's biggest challenge."

"In this case, Ben deserves a lot of credit for his department's performance improvement – he accepted the challenge. He believed enough in the coaching model to accept the profile he discovered of himself, weaknesses and all. The key thing, though, is that he chose to do something about it. Not everyone does."

Kitchell nods. "I'm looking forward to seeing the results of the pilot test. If it's positive, then I'll recommend we roll it out to all the managers – including the senior ones. How do you think Lester will react to that kind of suggestion?"

I raise my eyebrows. "Don't know, but it'll be fun to watch." I hesitate for a moment. "He's been on holiday for three weeks, so he'll be seeing the results at the same time you are."

The moment of truth has finally arrived. Except for Kitchell, every member of the Executive is present and waiting for me to start.

The President looks around and says, "James, why don't you start. Norma is going to be a few minutes late."

"Okay."

I turn on the overhead projector. "Good afternoon. The object of my presentation is to reveal the results of the coaching pilot test. As you know, we did a first survey back in March and a second survey just a week ago. Over one hundred employees – 10% of the workforce – participated in the survey; this is a significant sample size. Throughout this six-month period I worked very closely with the four test group managers, leaving the control group managers on their own. Here are the results."

Net change (%)	Test Group **With** Coaching	Control Group **Without** Coaching	Net Change **With** Coaching
Image	+6.3 %	-7.9 %	+14.2 %
Climate	+10.9 %	-3.5 %	+14.4 %
Credibility	+6.9 %	-4.4 %	+11.3 %
Desire to	+12.0 %	- 4.9 %	+16.9 %
Skills	+7.1 %	+1.0 %	+6.1 %
Capacity	+10.7 %	+1.5 %	+9.2 %
Average	**+8.98 %**	**-3.03 %**	**+12.0 %**

"What this means is that in this six-month period, the four test managers – those 'With Coaching' – showed a spectacular net average improvement of 12% over their colleagues – the 'Control Group.'"

I stop to let the information sink in.

Foggs, the Vice President of Finance, asks, "A net improvement in what?"

"A net improvement in performance indicators and principal factors that impact on productivity and profitability – in the long term." I reply.

Foggs fires back, "And what was the impact on the short term?"

"I can't tell you exactly for all, but the Customer Service foreman improved his department's productivity by over 40%! Meaning that he got 40% more jobs done and billed with less re-work than before. His counterpart in the control group wasn't even close.

The test group coaches in Sales, Warehousing and Welding showed marked improvements in each of their respective areas: for example, 'territory coverage' – number of customers calls – grew by 10%; 'shipment returns' because of wrong addressing decreased by 6%; and the Welding foreman improved his department's output by 4%."

Droubs jumps in and asks, "All because of the coaching?"

I hesitate for a moment. "That's what the scientific evidence showed us."

Cones, the President, interjects, "James, I'm impressed that over such a short period you were able to get these kind of results. Very impressive!"

Before I can react, Kitchell walks in. Cones turns to her and says, "Norma, like you thought, the results are very good!"

Kitchell nods. "So should we go ahead with what we've planned?"

Zaco sits up. "What plan?"

Cones and Kitchell look at each other, and Cones says, "We'd like to roll out the coaching program to all the managers – including ourselves."

"Great idea," Zaco says, but he doesn't look altogether happy.

Cones turns to me and says, "James, as of next Monday, I'd like you to start reporting directly to Norma. You'll move your office downstairs and begin evaluating all our managers, starting with us!"

Zaco is stunned. He turns to Cones. "Can I speak to you privately for a moment?"

Cones shakes his head impatiently. "I'd like to settle this first. You and I can meet afterwards." Then he turns to me. "James, I know this is sudden, but I guarantee you'll be happy with the working conditions and the increase in pay. What do you say?"

I'm still in shock. "But what about my current job as Training Manager?"

Kitchell: "I've talked it over with Tom Wunkler and he's ready to step in."

"Wait a minute!" Zaco snaps. "What do you mean you've just talked to Wunkler? He works for me! Not for you!" He glares at the President. "Hugh, what's going on here?"

Cones ignores the question and waves at Kitchell to continue. "I've just left Tom and he's agreed to it, if you agree to move down here."

I nod in agreement and turn to Zaco. "It's almost four o'clock," I say calmly. "Should I meet you at your office in 15 minutes?"

He's obviously distressed. "I want to meet with the President first; make it half an hour." He walks out of the room, trailing behind Cones.

〜〜〜

"Hi, boys! How was your first day at school?"

"Great!"

"Love my teacher!" says Max.

"Me too!" says Ty.

Personally, I'm not sure if it'll stay that way.

Charlene has just arrived herself and is picking up a coat here, a schoolbag there, trying to keep some order despite the chaos the boys have already caused in the few minutes they've been home. I walk behind her and give her a kiss.

She turns and grins. "Sweetie, you're home early! And you bought me a rose! What's the occasion?"

"Well, I've got some great news for you!"

"What is it?"

I explain the events of the day and my meeting with Zaco.

She stands shocked, glued to every word. Finally she asks, "And you gave Zaco a copy of what?"

I reach in my pocket and show her the audiotape.

She whoops and we both start laughing.

"And you know what else?"

"There's more?"

"I called your publisher friend. I'm meeting her next week!"

"That's phenomenal."

I give her another kiss. "You know…the kids are heading outside to play and dinner isn't due for another hour. What do you say?"

Charlene laughs and I follow her upstairs.

What About You? _____

• How would you now define "coaching"?

_____

_____

_____

_____

_____

• What are the key elements to a successful "coaching" implementation?

_____

_____

_____

_____

_____

178

TEST YOURSELF and your SUPERVISOR _____

Answer each statement according to the following scale:
Almost never - 1   Sometimes - 2   Regularly - 3   Almost always - 4

71. In your work group, people get
recognition for doing good work.   1   2   3   4

72. In your work group, new ideas are
listened to.   1   2   3   4

73. In your work group, people serve
customers in a way that builds and
maintains mutual trust and
confidence.   1   2   3   4

74. Today, your work group responds
better to customer needs than it did
six months ago.   1   2   3   4

Self-Learning Section

Assessments and Prescriptions

Preview

In this section you'll have the opportunity to evaluate your
coaching profile and/or that of your superior. You'll also get
suggestions on how to further develop your profile by following
some simple tips and completing written exercises in the
Self-Learning Modules at the end of the section.

Your Coaching Profile – Self-Evaluation

In order to self-assess your CREDIBILITY complete the following:

Write in the appropriate boxes the scores that you gave yourself:

Question #

#07 – score	____			
#09 – score	____			
#11 – score	____			
#22 – score	____			
#24 – score	____	Total Score ____		Average Score _____

If Average Score is greater than 2.5 ... you assess your overall CREDIBILITY as being good.

If Average Score is less than 2.5 ... you assess your overall CREDIBILITY as needing improvement and therefore some form of corrective action needs to be taken.

〰

Here are some suggestions:

- Select a team Captain – the group leader
- Read: *The Power of Ethical Management*
    By K. Blanchard & N.V. Peale (Fawcett Columbine, New York, 1998)
- Read: *Trust in the Balance*
    By R.B. Shaw (Jossey-Bass, San Francisco, 1997)
- Read: *Sacred Hoops, Spiritual Lessons of a Hardwood Warrior*
    By P. Jackson & H. Delahanty (Hyperion, New York, 1995)
- See the motion picture: *Eddie*
    By Hollywood Pictures, Polygram Filmed Entertainment/Island Picture Studio, 1996.

Your Coaching Profile – Self-Evaluation

In order to self-assess your DESIRE TO COACH complete the following:

Write in the appropriate boxes the scores that you gave yourself:

Question #

#15 – score   _____
#26 – score   _____
#51 – score   _____
#59 – score   _____
#61 – score   _____
#63 – score   _____   Total Score _____   Average Score _____

If Average Score is greater than 2.5 ... you assess your overall DESIRE TO COACH as being good.

If Average Score is less than 2.5 ... you assess your overall DESIRE TO COACH as needing improvement and therefore some form of corrective action needs to be taken.

〰️

Here are some suggestions:

• Read: *Self-Learning Module: Tips & Exercises for Rewarding Effective Coaching*
• Read: *Self-Learning Module: Tips & Exercises for Effective Interpersonal Communications*
• Read: *Self-Learning Module: Tips & Exercises for Getting More Capacity*
• Read: *Principles of Self-Management*
   By J.C. Marshall & B. McHardy (Self Management Group, Toronto, 1999)

Your Coaching Profile – Self-Evaluation

In order to self-assess your SKILLS TO COACH complete the following:

Write in the appropriate boxes the scores that you gave yourself:

Question #

#17 – score   _____
#19 – score   _____
#28 – score   _____
#30 – score   _____
#32 – score   _____
#34 – score   _____
#36 – score   _____
#38 – score   _____
#41 – score   _____
#43 – score   _____
#45 – score   _____
#47 – score   _____
#49 – score   _____   Total Score _____   Average Score _____

If Average Score is greater than 2.5 ... you assess your overall SKILLS as being good.

If Average Score is less than 2.5 ... you assess your overall SKILLS as needing improvement and therefore some form of corrective action needs to be taken.

〜

Here are some suggestions:

- Read: *Self-Learning Module: Tips & Exercises for Increasing Productivity*
- Read: *Self-Learning Module: Tips & Exercises for Effective Interpersonal Communications*
- Read: *Self-Learning Module: Tips & Exercises for Teaching Adults*

Your Coaching Profile – Self-Evaluation

In order to self-assess your CAPACITY TO COACH complete the following:

Write in the appropriate boxes the scores that you gave yourself:

Question #

#13 – score   _____
#55 – score   _____
#57 – score   _____
#65 – score   _____
#67 – score   _____
#69 – score   _____   Total Score _____   Average Score _____

If Average Score is greater than 2.5 ... you assess your overall CAPACITY as being good.

If Average Score is less than 2.5 ... you assess your overall CAPACITY as being a problem and therefore some form of corrective action needs to be taken.

〰

Here are some suggestions:

- Read: *Self-Learning Module: Tips & Exercises for Getting More Capacity*
- Read: *The Goal*
    By E.M. Goldratt (North River Press, 1992)
- Read: *The One Minute Manager*
    By K. Blanchard & S. Johnson (Berkley Books, New York, 1982).
- Read: *The 7 Habits of Highly Effective People*
    By S.R. Covey (Fireside, New York, 1989)

Your Superior's Coaching Profile – Evaluation

In order to assess your superior's CREDIBILITY complete the following:

Write in the appropriate boxes the scores that you gave for:

Question #

#08 – score   ____

#10 – score   ____

#12 – score   ____

#23 – score   ____

#25 – score   ____   Total Score ____   Average Score _____

If Average Score is greater than 2.5 ... you assess your superior's overall CREDIBILITY as being good.

If Average Score is less than 2.5 ... you assess your superior's overall CREDIBILITY as needing improvement and therefore some form of corrective action needs to be taken.

In order to assess your superior's DESIRE TO COACH complete the following:

Write in the appropriate boxes the scores you gave for:

Question #

#16 – score   ____

#27 – score   ____

#52 – score   ____

#60 – score   ____

#62 – score   ____

#64 – score   ____   Total Score ____   Average Score _____

If Average Score is greater than 2.5 ... you assess your superior's overall DESIRE TO COACH as being good.

If Average Score is less than 2.5 ... you assess your superior's overall DESIRE TO COACH as needing improvement and therefore some form of corrective action needs to be taken.

In order to assess your superior's SKILLS TO COACH complete the following:

Write in the appropriate boxes the scores that you gave for:

Question #

#18 – score   ____   #37 – score   ____
#20 – score   ____   #39 – score   ____
#29 – score   ____   #42 – score   ____
#31 – score   ____   #44 – score   ____
#33 – score   ____   #46 – score   ____
#35 – score   ____   #48 – score   ____
#50 – score   ____

Total Score   ____   Average Score _____

If Average Score is greater than 2.5 ... you assess your superior's overall SKILLS as being good.

If Average Score is less than 2.5 ... you assess your superior's overall SKILLS as needing improvement and therefore some form of corrective action needs to be taken.

In order to assess your superior's CAPACITY TO COACH complete the following:

Write in the appropriate boxes the scores that you gave for:

Question #

#14 – score   ____
#56 – score   ____
#58 – score   ____
#66 – score   ____
#68 – score   ____
#70 – score   ____   Total Score _____   Average Score _____

If Average Score is greater than 2.5 ... you assess your superior's overall CAPACITY as being good.

If Average Score is less than 2.5 ... you assess your superior's overall CAPACITY as being a problem and therefore some form of corrective action needs to be taken.

Self-Learning Section

Tips & Exercises

Preview

The following modules were designed to provide you with specific tips and exercises to further your coaching development:

- Tips & Exercises for Increasing Productivity
- Tips & Exercises for Teaching Adults
- Tips & Exercises for Effective Interpersonal Communications
- Tips & Exercises for Getting More Capacity
- Tips & Exercises for Rewarding Effective Coaching

Tips & Exercises

for

Increasing Productivity

Learning Objective

To improve your coaching effectiveness in the skills areas of 'goal setting,' 'organization/anticipation,' 'preparation' and 'delegation.'

Overview

The goal of every profit organization is to make money – to maximize net profit. The most successful organizations whether they're manufacturing- or service-based, do it by following three rules:

- Maximizing 'throughput' – the rate of productivity at which a system generates money through sales.
- Minimizing 'inventory' – all the money that the system has invested in purchasing things that it intends to sell.
- Minimizing 'operational expenses' – all the money the system spends in order to turn inventory into throughput.

(Source: *The Goal*, by E.M.Goldratt, North River Press, 1992):

In each organization there are many sub-systems that contribute directly to the organization's overall throughput. In fact, the rate of productivity of each sub-system has a direct impact on the overall rate of productivity or through-put of the organization. Here are some examples:

- The rate at which the Accounting department processes an invoice (e.g. gather the information (contract, customer agreement), generate the invoice, send invoice to customer, collect payment from customer, deposit receipts in bank)

- The rate at which the Shipping department delivers a product (e.g. gather information, get material, package material for transport, load material, ship it)
- The rate at which the Sales force obtains a customer agreement (e.g. learn marketing strategy, learn products/services being offered, understand market (territory), contact customer, uncover customer needs, present products/services, get agreement, report on sales call, follow-up with customer)
- The rate at which the Training department delivers a program (conduct needs analysis, assign resources, develop program content, deliver program, evaluate results)
- The rate at which components are assembled into a finished product (e.g. gather information (job order), assign resources, get components, assemble components, store finished product)

Minimizing inventory and operating expenses also apply at the sub-system level. Whether it's raw material in manufacturing or raw data in a service industry, as inventory moves through the various sub-systems in an organization, the expenses associated with processing it must be minimized. So too must the investment in acquiring and holding the inventory – whether it be 'information' or 'product' – be minimized. Important information sitting on someone's desk can be as costly to an organization as parts sitting in a warehouse – if not more!

What this means is that effective managers/coaches generate the maximum productivity with the minimum of investment, or to put it differently, get the most out of the department's structures, processes and resources. It also means continually evaluating the activities being done in order to ensure an optimal flow of activities.

Constraints

Unfortunately, most organizational sub-systems are laden with activities that slow down the process (cycle of activities), creating blockages called 'bottlenecks.' They can have a crippling effect on the rate of profitability by severely impacting 'throughput,' 'inventory' and 'operational expenses.'

Activities that create bottlenecks can be easily spotted — just look for piles or line-ups of things. The activity just ahead of the bottleneck is usually the culprit – it can be stacks of paper, piles of products or line-ups of people.

191

Sometimes the bottleneck is created within the department and sometimes from outside – in the case where a department is dependent on another to provide an 'input' before it can move forward. The result of a bottleneck is that the overall system's capacity to produce is limited by the capacity of the bottleneck. What this means is that the bottleneck is the most critical factor in setting productivity rates for the system. It also means that the loss of productivity because of a bottleneck can never be recovered by the system – all else being equal.

TIPS

In order to *anticipate* problems, effectively *organize* the activities of the system and prepare a strategy, the manager/coach should:

1. List, in sequence, the cycle of activities (sub-system) of the department from start to finish.
2. Determine which activities slow down the process – the bottlenecks.
3. Generate a strategy to manage the bottleneck and increase the rate of productivity.

A cycle in a sub-system is completed only after all the activities are done. So, for example, in a cycle of twenty activities, even if eighteen can be completed quickly, the process isn't over until the remaining two are done. Sometimes the slowest activity is the first one in the process; sometimes it's the last one. Regardless whether the slowest activity (bottleneck) is first, second or last, the output or rate of productivity is the same.

So obviously, the best course of action is to eliminate the activity from the entire system, if possible. Another alternative is to increase the bottleneck's capacity. This can be done by weighing the costs of adding new 'outside' resources to the activity, versus the productivity gains. If you bring in an 'inside' resource (already in your sub-system) make sure you're not creating a new bottleneck at the point where the 'inside' resource comes from.

If neither one of these options is possible, follow these 3 tips:

1. Make sure that there is never any 'down time' in a bottleneck. It should never be idle or stopped for whatever reason. Remember that a sub-system produces only as fast (productive) as its slowest activity (bottleneck).
2. Make sure that only the essential inputs go into the bottleneck. Don't

waste important processing time and capacity by including inputs or elements that aren't absolutely necessary. Sometimes moving the bottleneck up or down the sequence of activities will make a system more efficient. For example, a 'quality control' activity is oftentimes a bottleneck and should usually be at the end of the cycle where the probability of 'rejects' is much lower; presumably, most of the 'bugs' have already been fixed and only high quality products reach the activity.

3. Because large batches generally create backlogs, when possible, process small batches in a bottleneck. It's usually more efficient.

EXERCISE

List your department's cycle of activities by writing down the primary activities (max. 10) in chronological sequence (from the first to the last).

1. _____

2. _____

3. _____

4. _____

5. _____

6. _____

7. _____

8. _____

9. _____

10. _____

EXERCISE

Identify the 2 slowest activities (bottlenecks) in your system. Explain why.

_____

_____

_____

_____

_____

_____

EXERCISE

Review the sequence of activities and write down a strategy for managing the bottleneck.

_____

_____

_____

What if you're the bottleneck?

What do you do if the stacks, piles, or line-ups are on your desk or in front of your door?

Exercise 1

List the activity/activities that is/are creating the bottleneck.

1. _____
2. _____
3. _____
4. _____
5. _____

Exercise 2

- **Ask yourself:** "Does this activity really contribute to the GOAL (e.g. making money)?"
- If the answer is **NO**, then eliminate it from the cycle.
- If the answer is **YES**, ask yourself: "Am I the only person who can do it?"
- If the answer is **YES**, spend as much time as possible completing the activity. You can increase your capacity to do this activity by reviewing other activities that are not directly related to the goal and are time-consuming. Here are some other tips:
  - **Do things differently** – Is there a more efficient way to do it?
  - **Group activities together** – Can I 'batch' this activity in with something else?
  - **Do it right away** – Can it be taken care of on the fly?
  - **Keep it simple** – Can I simplify the activity? Fewer steps maybe?

- **Set time limits** – What's the maximum amount of time I will spend on the activity?
- **Increase your competency** – Would training help me do a better job?
- If the answer is **NO**, then **DELEGATE** the task to someone else. (Beware: moving a bottleneck elsewhere in the system doesn't ensure an increase in the rate of productivity. Be sure to move the activity to an area where there's more capacity to complete the task. In other words, give it to someone who may have more time or be better suited to complete the task effectively and efficiently).

Exercise 3

a) In the 1st column of the Table, list your activities in the system;

b) In the 2nd column, check off the activities that are creating bottlenecks; and

c) In the 3rd column, decide on an immediate action step

Activities (in chronological sequence)	Bottlenecks (✓)	Action Steps
1.		
2.		
3.		
4.		
5.		
6.		
7.		
8.		
9.		
10.		

Quiz

1. 'Throughput' is:
   a) The rate of growth in an organization
   b) The rate of productivity of a system
   c) The rate of employee turnover
   d) The rate of thoroughness

2. 'Inventory' and 'Expenses' in a system should be:
   a) Maximized
   b) Minimized
   c) Equalized
   d) Proportioned

3. Bottlenecks in a system can be found by:
   a) Looking for defective materials
   b) Looking for large groups of people
   c) Looking for line-ups or stacks of things
   d) Looking for narrow spaces

4. True or False
   a) The best way to manage a bottleneck is to
      eliminate it   T____ F____
   b) Make sure there's plenty of 'down time'
      in the bottleneck   T____ F____
   c) Make sure that only the essential inputs go
      into a bottleneck   T____ F____
   d) Try to process large batches in a bottleneck –
      it's more efficient   T____ F____

5. If you're responsible for an activity that's creating a bottleneck, you
   should:
   a) Bring the work home
   b) Find someone else to do it
   c) Keep it for the end of the day when you won't be interrupted
   d) Decide if the activity is absolutely necessary, if you're the only per-
      son that can accomplish it, or if it can be delegated to someone
      with more capacity than you

Answer key: 1-b; 2-b; 3-c; 4-T,F,T,F; 5-d

Tips & Exercises

for

Teaching Adults

Learning Objective

To increase your coaching skills by improving your 'teaching' and 'practicing' abilities.

Overview

The following paragraphs from M. Knowles's excellent book, *The Adult Learner: A neglected species* (Gulf Publishing Co.), describe the sad history of adult education:

"Considering that the education of adults has been a concern of the human race for a very long time, it's curious that there has been so little thinking, investigating, and writing about adult learning until recently. The adult learner has indeed been a neglected species.

This is especially surprising in view of the fact that all of the great teachers of ancient times were all teachers of adults, not children. For example, Confucius and Lao Tse of China; the Hebrew prophets and Jesus in Biblical times; Aristotle, Socrates, and Plato in ancient Greece; and Cicero, Evelid, and Quintillian in ancient Rome. Because their experience was with adults, they came to have a very different concept of the learning/teaching process from the one that later came to dominate formal education. They perceived learning to be a process of active inquiry, not passive reception of transmitted content. Accordingly, they invented techniques for actively engaging learners in inquiry. The ancient Chinese and Hebrews invented what we would now call the case method, in which the leader or one of the group members would describe a situation, often in the form of a parable, and jointly they would explore its characteristics and possible resolutions.

The Greeks invented what we now call the Socratic dialogue, in which the leader or a group member would pose a question or dilemma and the group members would pool their thinking and experience in seeking an answer or solution. The Romans were more confrontational: they used challenges that forced group members to state positions and then defend them.

Starting in the seventh century in Europe, schools began being organized for teaching children – primarily for preparing young boys for the priesthood – hence they became known as cathedral and monastic schools. Since the teachers in these schools had as their principal mission the indoctrination of students in the beliefs, faith, and rituals of the Church, they evolved a set of assumptions about learning and strategies for teaching that came to be labeled 'pedagogy.' This model of education persisted through the ages well into the twentieth century and was the basis of organization of our entire educational system.

Starting shortly after the end of World War I, there began emerging both in this country and Europe a growing body of notions about the unique characteristics of adults as learners. But only in the last decades have these notions evolved into a comprehensive theory of adult learning."

TIPS

- Children are mostly interested in their test **scores** – Adults are mostly interested in **applying what they learn**.
- Children are very **dependent** on the teacher – Adults are more **independent** of the teacher.
- Past experience is **not important** to the child learner – Past experience is **very important** to the adult learner.
- For children, much of the **desire** to learn comes **from the teacher** – For adults, much of the **desire** to learn comes **from within**.
- For children, the learning is directed at the **subject** – For adults, the learning is directed at the **problem**.

7 Conditions to Successful Learning for an Adult

1. They must **want to learn**.
2. They must **understand the reason** for learning something.
3. They must be **solving realistic problems** through the use of learning experiences.
4. They must receive **contingent re-enforcement** through **balanced feedback**.

5. They must feel **comfortable** (no fear of failure) in applying the new learning.
6. They must take some **responsibility in planning and implementing** their learning activities.
7. The organizational **context must be comfortable** – people feel confident and have mutual respect for one another, willing to help each other, are free to express their views, and accept diversity.

TIPS

- Be **ready** – master the **subject content**. Continually **learn** about it.
- Be **enthusiastic** about teaching to others – the desire to teach breeds confidence in the students.
- Enjoy **being around people** – radiate warmth
- Don't **preach**. Use the **self-discovery** approach – create and present situations in which the other person discovers the answers on his or her own.
- Be **focused** – **eliminate distractions** by securing the appropriate amount of capacity (time, space and materials).
- Have participants practice, practice and practice.

EXERCISE

Describe an upcoming situation where you're called upon to teach another adult (who, what, why).

_____

_____

_____

What will you do to ensure that the desired behavioural change occurs?

_____

_____

_____

_____

_____

Tips & Exercises

for

Effective Interpersonal

Communications

Learning Objective

These tips will help you improve your 'interpersonal communication skills' and coaching effectiveness in 'relating to others.' It'll also help you be more comfortable and effective in consulting with 'subordinates' or providing 'contingent re-enforcement.'

Overview

Effective interpersonal communication is a process that can be learned. It's as much the result of managing the mood as it is the words. Because one affects the other and ultimately the outcome, it's important to understand and be sensitive to both.

S.E.E.C.

S.E.E.C. is a structured approach to ensure that the purpose, the exchange and the outcomes of a discussion are clearly understood and delivered in a climate that is respectful of each person.

1. **Start**
2. **Explore**
3. **Explain**
4. **Close**

Start

A conversation should begin by talking about issues that are general and unthreatening (e.g. news, weather, sports). Gradually the discussion should move towards more specific issues relating to the discussion (e.g. business situation and purpose of the meeting). For example:

Opening statements (general):

> Coach says: "Hi Jane! How are you?"
>
> Employee responds: "Pretty good. But the weather is starting to get to me."
>
> Coach says: "I know what you mean. All this rain is starting to get to me too."

Statement of purpose (specific):

> Coach says: "Jane, the reason I wanted to meet with you was to find out a little more about your approach to managing difficult customers. It'll help me better understand the issues. And in the end help each other."
>
> Employee responds: "Sure. What would you like to know?"

Explore and Explain

In the course of a conversation, you move back and forth between *exploring* (obtaining information) and *explaining* (giving information).

Typically, people are more inclined to give information than receive it. So asking the right kinds of questions to obtain information is a critical step in understanding the issues and establishing a climate of mutual respect and openness. Business discussions sometimes move from a *positive comfort zone* to a *negative comfort zone*. Be mindful of which zone you're in or about to enter – it'll influence the way you ask and respond to questions.

- Especially at the beginning, use *comfortable open-ended questions* to get the other person to talk freely and elaborate – questions that begin with why, what, how. It prevents the conversation from turning into an inquisition and promotes a true dialogue.
- Confirm your understanding of what the other person has said by using *closed-ended questions* – questions that the other person will respond to with a 'yes' or 'no.' For example, "So what your saying is…Is that it?"

- If you ask a question, always respond to the answer with a nod, "I see" or "Go on." Keep your **emotional reactions** in check. If you feel an emotional reaction coming on, ask another question. For example:

  Employee says: "I don't think that'll work."

  Coach says: "Can you tell me more?" or "Please, go on..."

- As you get deeper into the conversation and might be entering a negative comfort zone, be **tactful** and **sensitive** in your approach. For example:

  Coach asks: "I'm afraid I have to ask you. Is there a problem with your driver's license?"

  If the other person reacts negatively, or doesn't want to answer, react by explaining: "I see this is a delicate matter for you. I respect your feelings here and so if you'd prefer to stop this discussion we can pick it up another time" or "I know this isn't easy for you, and I want to help. But I believe we need to address this issue. Otherwise, the problem is going to persist and that's not a good situation for you or the organization. What do you think?"

- If you make a statement, always **ask for a response**. For example, "What do you think?" or "What are your feelings about this?" Be prepared to listen intently.

- **Practice using pauses in your conversations.** Give the other person a chance to fill the silence. It shows you're listening and interested in wanting to hear more. It also gives the other person the opportunity to complete his/her thoughts or adjust the statement he/she just made. For example:

  Employee says: "I don't think that'll work."

  Coach says nothing – (Pause for a few seconds)

  Employee continues: "What I mean is that the timing isn't good for that kind of proposal."

- If the other person has exceeded your performance expectations, recognize it quickly by **explaining the specific attributes or skills used** and the impact on the organization. For example:

Coach says: "Mary, I'm impressed with your recent work at ABC. Your ability to overcome objections and your persistence in following-up with them has resulted in a 15% gain in new business. Thanks for being such a good example to the others."

Close

An effective close to a discussion involves a **summary** of what's been said: review of purpose, issues raised, areas of agreement and disagreement, and finally the next steps. For example:

Coach says: "Let's recap. This meeting was set up to decide on a course of action regarding territory coverage. We both agree that coverage is important but you feel that because of the size of your territory, you're forced to travel long distances in short periods of time. The result has been several speeding tickets and you're one ticket away from losing your license. So you want a smaller territory or do inside sales for a while. Right?"

Employee says: "Yes. I need to get off the road for a while."

- **If you agree**, close the discussion by confirming what's been said by restating it with a question. For example:

Coach confirms: "OK. We'll temporarily assign you to an inside sales position and review the situation in six months. Is that OK with you?"

- **If an agreement can't be reached** and you're not willing to explore other alternatives, close the discussion by stating that you respect the other person's point of view and that in the interest of the organization you've decided on another course of action.

Coach says: "I understand that by taking you off the road you wouldn't feel the pressure of having to rush to those outlying customers. But unfortunately, there are no inside sales positions available and besides, we need you in the field. I'd like you to participate in a Territory Management training program that'll give you some ideas on how to manage your territory more efficiently. If you still feel that this isn't enough, we'll assign you to a much smaller territory, which unfortunately for you, would mean much smaller commissions. Are you okay with this?"

TIPS

Don't assume

The most common mistake in communication is assuming you know what the other person is thinking. Always clarify and confirm your assumptions. For example:

> Coach makes an assumption and says to his superior: "You're really busy – things must be going well!"

> The superior responds: "Not really. We've just had to lay off several people from other divisions in order to protect our overall profitability. So your timing for a meeting is not very good."

A BETTER WAY OF SAYING IT WOULD BE...

> Coach says: "You seem really busy – how are things going?"

Be clear

The biggest challenge for most people, whether it's face-to-face or in a group setting, is clarity. Keep ideas simple, concise and if possible back it up with a visual aid or an example. For example:

> Coach says: "The department's in trouble. I think part of the problem is the way we're organized. Any ideas how we can do it better?"

A BETTER WAY OF SAYING IT WOULD BE...

> Coach says: "The department's productivity is dropping. I think part of the problem is the growing number of bottlenecks in the system. Any ideas how we can manage them better? Here, take a look at this flowchart."

> Coach says: "Have you heard about the layoffs? Things are getting pretty tight everywhere. My brother-in-law got laid off a few weeks back – he had a position like yours – his wife's income is all that's left…"

> Employee responds: "I'm sorry to hear that, but I've got to get back to work. Wish him luck!"

> Coach says: "Harry! Wait! I'm telling you this for a reason! Harry…!"

204

A BETTER WAY OF SAYING IT WOULD BE...

Coach says: "Harry, I'm afraid that because of the economic down-turn we've been asked to cut back on head count. I'd like to discuss with you what this means for our department and look at ways on how to avoid laying anyone off."

Keep an open mind

The strongest attitude to guard against is a closed mind to someone else's point of view. The inability to understand or unwillingness to try to understand will close down a conversation very quickly. For example:

Employee says: "The work schedule isn't working."

Coach responds (closed mind): "It's working in other areas."

A BETTER WAY OF SAYING IT WOULD BE...

Coach responds: "Oh? Why is that?"

Employee responds: "We're short of staff and people are getting tired."

Coach responds (closed mind): "No one else is having the problem."

A BETTER WAY OF SAYING IT WOULD BE...

Coach responds: " Tell me more."

Employee says: "You've got to make some changes, this isn't working."

Coach responds (closed mind): "But it should work..."

A BETTER WAY OF SAYING IT WOULD BE...

Coach responds: "What do you think the problem is?" or " Any suggestions?"

Control your advice

Be careful about giving advice when it's not needed or sought. Get your facts straight. Otherwise you might be saying things that will undermine your credibility. For example:

Coach says: "Joe, what you need is something to improve your attitude. How about some training sessions?"

Other person responds: "Get real! I'm already taking over 100 hours of training per year just to keep up with new technology!"

Coach replies: "Oh."

A BETTER WAY OF SAYING IT WOULD BE...

Coach says: " Joe, you don't seem very happy. Is there anything I can do to help you?"

EXERCISE

One of your top performers is not participating in a new incentive program that you know will be good for the business. You don't understand why. Using S.E.E.C., what kind of questions and statements would you use to keep the climate constructive?

_____

_____

_____

EXERCISE

Describe a past situation where you:

a) Made false assumptions. Why?

_____

_____

_____

b) Discovered that your explanation was unclear. Why?

_____

_____

_____

c) Had a closed mind to another's opinion. Why?

_____

_____

_____

d) Gave advice without sufficient information. Why?

_____

_____

_____

Quiz

1. You should start a discussion by:
   a) Immediately getting to the point
   b) Describing your dissatisfaction
   c) Talking about general issues
   d) Asking questions

2. S.E.E.C. stands for:
   a) Search, Explore, Eliminate, Contact
   b) Seek, Examine, Explain, Control
   c) Stop, Explore, Explain, Confirm
   d) Start, Explore, Explain, Close

3. Using open-ended questions will encourage people to:
   a) Request information
   b) Give information
   c) Gather information
   d) Analyze information

4. Before asking delicate questions you should ensure that:
   a) The climate is right
   b) There's nothing left to say
   c) The other person is sitting
   d) There's someone else in the room

5. If you make a statement, always ask for:
   a) A commitment
   b) A response to the statement
   c) A promise never to repeat it
   d) An agreement

Answer key: 1-c; 2-d; 3-b; 4-a; 5-b

```
┌─────────────────────────────────────────────┐
│                                               │
│           Tips & Exercises                    │
│                                               │
│                 for                           │
│                                               │
│        Getting More Capacity                  │
│                                               │
└─────────────────────────────────────────────┘
```

Learning Objective

How many times have you heard, "I don't have time to coach my people!" or "I can't afford it!" or "I need some support – materials" or "Where am I supposed to do this?" Lack of resources is the most often mentioned reason for not coaching, and a legitimate barrier.

In this module, you'll learn how to improve your coaching effectiveness for getting more CAPACITY (time, information, management support, space, and money) by using proven **sales** and **negotiating** techniques. If you need to go to your boss for more capacity, your chances of succeeding will be greatly improved if you make your case like a salesmen pitches a product to a customer – by presenting benefits that respond to a clearly defined need. The sale of your idea is not always guaranteed so you must be ready with a plan to compromise (negotiate) – only if necessary.

PART I: Selling the IDEA

Some of the best and worst sales people have never taken a sales course in their lives. How can this be? The answer is simple – good sales people whether they've been trained or not, have at least three things in common:

- They know their stuff (product, service, idea)
- They think and feel what the other person is thinking and feeling
- They usually find a way to reach an agreement without giving away the store

Know what you're selling

Whether it's in an informal or formal setting, you never want to be told, "You don't know what you're talking about!" or "I think you'd better get your facts straight." You want people to think and say, "He really knows his stuff."

Information is power. And the absolutely best way to be credible and build a relationship based on competence and confidence is to know what you're selling inside and out. This means getting the existing facts through research, or generating new facts through trials.

TIP

Understand the features and benefits of the resources you need in order to coach your people effectively. Write out exactly what you need and how it's going to increase the productivity and/or the profitability of the organization. Provide evidence or proof. For example:

> Coach says: "Because of the many and constant changes, I need at least 4 full days a month to meet one-on-one with my 10 people. This will ensure that they understand and apply the policies and practices of the organization."

Feature	Benefit to Organization	Proof
1. 4 days / month or 3 hrs / employee Time to evaluate (test) their technical knowledge and if necessary to help them in finding a way to acquire new information	• Increased customer satisfaction (fewer errors in giving out information) • Increased productivity (faster service therefore more customers can be processed) • Increased profitability (fewer mistakes + more customers = more sales = more profits)	• Statistics regarding customer satisfaction surveys • Productivity reports of competent employees versus those that are technically challenged • Cost of fixing mistakes versus doing it right the first time

Know how to sell face-to-face

Every idea-selling session should have a framework that will guide you in the discussion process. Use the S.E.E.C. process discussed in *Tips and Exercises for Effective Interpersonal Communications.*

TIP

Start a discussion in a *comfort zone* by talking about issues that are general and non-threatening. Next, **Explore** for information and feelings. You can do this by inviting the other person to talk about what's important to them; use *open* questions to get the other person to elaborate, *closed* questions to clarify and confirm the other person's point, and be conscious of the *comfort zones*. Once the situation is clearly understood, get *permission to* **Explain** your idea for more CAPACITY – a potential *discomfort zone*. Remember, **don't assume**, be **clear**, and keep an **open mind**. The best way to do this is by asking a question that links the other person's needs to the benefits of your idea. For example:

> Other person says: "So as you can see, our profits are well below plan."

> Coach says: "If I showed you that – with more time to coach my people – we could increase our department's profitability, would you be willing to listen to a proposal?"

If the other person expresses interest in the idea, then present the features and benefits of 'more time to coach your people.' For example:

> Coach says: "If I could get 4 days a month to devote myself entirely to coaching my people, I believe I could significantly increase our productivity and profitability."

> Other person asks: "How's that?"

> Coach says: "As you know, with the huge quantity of information we get and the rate at which it keeps changing, it's very difficult for our people to discriminate the 'nice to know' versus 'the need to know' information. Our productivity depends on our ability to manage the right information. I think I can help them to become more efficient, with 3 hrs/month of 'one-on-one' coaching. I'll assess their knowledge level to make sure that they're competent in the areas that are most critical to our business – the 'need-to-know' information; if I discover gaps, then I'll suggest some form of corrective action. By doing this, we'll cut down on mistakes, increase our productivity rates and make more money. What do you think?"

Get the *commitment* by summarizing how the proposal will meet the needs of the organization and what action steps you're going to take. For example:

> Coach says: "Let me summarize what we agreed to. First, I'll devote 4 full days per month in one-on-one coaching with my people. In order to free up the time, you agree that I pass on some of my current activities to someone else. I'll approach the IS department today to see if they can take over some of these other activities. Okay?"

Know how to overcome negative 'attitudes'

In a 'proposal' scenario there are usually 4 types of negative attitudes that can surface:

1. Skepticism – an attitude where the other person likes the idea but doubts it'll work. For example:

> Coach says: "I'll approach the IS department today to see if they can take over some of these other activities. Okay?"

> Other person's reaction: "I still have my doubts about the benefits of your proposal!"

TIP

This attitude usually shows up right after you've presented your proposal and are trying to get a commitment. The best way to overcome 'skepticism' is to **offer evidence (proof) that it works**. Obviously, this means that you've prepared your proof sources before the meeting. If the proof doesn't exist, conduct a 'trial' on your own and present the results. Or, suggest to the other person that you 'pilot test' the idea first – this minimizes the exposure to a lot of costs before the idea is implemented. For example:

> Other person says: "I don't see how this idea will increase our sales."

> You offer credible proof by saying: "Here are the results of a survey conducted in our industry where it clearly shows that more coaching can boost sales by up to 70%!"

2. Indifference – an attitude where the other person has no interest in your plan – sees no need. For example:

> You say: "I have an idea that'll increase the amount of time I spend with the sales force. I'd like to talk to you about it."

Other person's 'indifference': "I don't really have time for this right now."

TIP

This attitude usually shows up at the beginning of the discussion. Right from the start you'll see, hear or feel that the other person is not interested in your idea. The best way to get them interested is to **strike a nerve with a provocative question**. For example:

Other person says: "I don't see the need to get this done right now."

Coach asks: "With the rumours about the company not making its profit numbers, do you think we'll be needing to put more pressure on our sales people in the next quarter?"

or

"Did you hear about the increase in market share our competitors are getting? They're saying it's because of a new field program they're implementing for their managers."

3. **False Objection Due to a Misunderstanding** – an attitude where the other person objects to something about your idea based on inaccurate information. For example:

Other person says: "We can't just eliminate reporting activities."

TIP

This attitude usually shows up at the end of your discussion, just after you've asked for a commitment. The other person probably likes your idea, but because of a perceived obstacle, isn't ready to commit to it. The best way to overcome this is by **explaining your understanding of the other person's concern and clearing it up with the *right* information**. For example:

Coach says: "You're right – we can't eliminate the weekly reports. What I'm saying is that if I gather the pertinent data and get IS to organize it in a functional and easier-to-understand format, I would save a full day of paperwork per week which would allow me to spend more time in the field coaching my sales people."

4. **True Objection** – an attitude that is the result of a legitimate problem. For example:

Coach says: "I suggest that we get IS involved by the end of the month."

Other person says: "IS is already up to their eyeballs with projects. I don't see how they can do it."

TIP

This attitude also usually shows up at the end of your discussion, just after you've asked for a commitment. The other person probably likes your idea, but because of a *real* obstacle, isn't ready to commit to it. The best way to overcome this is by **re-iterating the benefits of your idea to remind them of what's to gain**. For example:

Coach says: "It's true that this'll require a re-shuffling of activities, but given the potential for field coaching to increase our sales by up to 70%, don't you think that this project should become a priority for IS? Or do you think that an outside agency could provide a similar service and benefit?"

EXERCISE

Write down a situation where you met someone with an *indifferent* attitude. How did you handle the situation?

_____

_____

_____

EXERCISE

You'll soon be meeting with your superior to present a new idea that will dramatically change the way you manage your team. You know there's going to be a lot of resistance on his or her part. What are three things you can do to meet the anticipated objections?

_____

_____

_____

_____

_____

_____

PART II: Negotiating the IDEA

Negotiating is another word for compromise. The best sales people ONLY negotiate AFTER all attempts to overcome the other person's objections have failed – NEVER BEFORE. If the other person will not accept your proposal – no matter what benefit you think it has – be prepared to reach an agreement through *compromise*.

EXERCISE

Recall the last time you were in a situation of having to negotiate with another person as a result of trying to convince him or her of your point of view. What did you give up? What did you gain?

_____

_____

_____

_____

_____

TIP

BE READY

If you believe there's a possibility that you might have to negotiate:

a) Get a sense of the values of the *things* that might be exchanged. Think about this before you present your initial idea. For example, what's the value of your time? Is the time you spend coaching your people worth the same as writing management reports? Does the other person perceive the same value? If not, why?

Typically, *things* you negotiate are *terms* and *conditions* NOT *outcomes*. Remember that if the other person has raised a legitimate objection, it means that they like your idea and the potential outcomes but aren't ready to commit to it because of some term or condition that's attached to the idea.

b) Know your limits of *give* and *take*. Think about *what* (term or condition) and *how much* of it you are prepared to **give**, in return to **receive** what you want. This will establish the range of alternatives you're prepared to consider. Compromise on terms of less value to you for terms that are crucial. For example, you might be willing to continue writing the weekly reports if the other person agrees to provide you with some organizational support to complete them (e.g. getting IS to design a template where the reports can be done more easily and downloaded from remote locations).

c) **Know the other person**. What are their personal and professional needs. Do they usually seek power and control? Are they risk-takers? Do they have a need for safety? Does money, recognition or performance drive them? Understanding their personality profile will help you in deciding what and how to present to them.

GET SET

- **Get a conditional agreement from the other person**. Before attempting to negotiate, make sure that the other person agrees that if you overcome the objection (terms and conditions) that's been raised, then you can proceed with the idea. For example:

  Coach says: "**If** we can find a way to resolve this difference (e.g. terms and conditions), will you **then** agree to give me the OK to proceed?"

GO

- **Offer the best-case compromise for *you***. Propose 'what you want' (optimum capacity), 'what you'll give' (minimum investment on your part), and 'what the expected outcome' will be. For example:

  Coach says: "If you give me 5 full days a month to coach my people, I'll meet with the IS department to develop a process to do the reports so that they can be submitted once a month. With this, I'm prepared to sign off on a new plan to increase our sales by 10% by year-end. What do you think?"

- **Agree to a best-case compromise for *both***. Propose 'what you want' (acceptable capacity), 'what you'll give' (acceptable investment), and 'what the expected outcome' will be. For example:

  Coach says: "If you give me 4 full days a month to coach my people, I'll meet with the IS department to develop a process to do the reports so that they can be submitted twice a month. With this, I'm prepared to sign off on a new plan to increase our sales by 15% by year-end. What do you think?"

OTHER things to remember:

- Never give anything away without getting something back in return
- Look for something of value to the other person that he or she might be willing to trade for and is completely outside of the specific proposal
- As a final option, offer to meet him/her halfway

STOP

- **NEVER AGREE to terms and conditions that you can't meet.** Sometimes due to misunderstanding, confusion or even intimidation, we accept terms and conditions that are beyond our limits. For example:

  Boss says: "I'll give you 2 full days, but in return you'll submit your reports every ten days and agree to sign off on a new plan of a 25% increase in sales."

  Coach says: "As much as I'd like to agree with that, I'm afraid I can't. Without the capacity (time) I'm looking for, I think we all lose – I won't be able to give enough coaching to my people and in the end, the department won't meet the new numbers you're talking about. So why bother? Why not leave things the way they are for now and agree to meet again in say a month?"

EXERCISE

Recall a negotiation where you were put into the position of having to 'walk away.' Were there further negotiations with this person at a later date? How did you handle them at that time?

_____

_____

_____

_____

_____

_____

```
┌─────────────────────────────────────────────┐
│                                               │
│          Tips & Exercises                     │
│                                               │
│                  for                          │
│                                               │
│      Rewarding Effective Coaching             │
│                                               │
└─────────────────────────────────────────────┘
```

Learning Objective

The DESIRE TO coach is directly linked to the rewards it provides the manager. Without some form of personal benefit (increased compensation or recognition), a manager will not be motivated to undertake necessary supervisory tasks that might sometimes be unpleasant.

This module will give you some insight into how 'Reward Systems' are designed by many North American organizations. It's intended to help you prepare a logical and convincing argument to increase the level of reward that should be attached to 'effective coaching,' and consequently have an impact on your constant DESIRE TO coach – in all situations.

Overview

The strategic purposes of 'Reward Systems' are to:

- **Attract potential job applicants** by assuring that the rewards are sufficient to attract the right people at the right time for the right jobs
- **Retain good employees** by offering internally equitable and competitive rewards
- **Motivate employees** by tying rewards to performance

There are 5 basic reward types. The relative importance of each type will depend on management's strategic plans and the individual employee's needs.

1. **Monetary:** Pay • Pay raise • Stock options • Profit sharing • Bonus Plans • Christmas bonus • Provision and use of company facilities • Deferred compensation, including other tax shelters • Pay and time-off for attending work-related training programs and seminars.

2. **Fringe Benefits:** Medical and Group Insurance Plan • Company physical exams • Company automobile • Desktop/Laptop/Palm computers • Pension contributions • Product discount plans • Vacation trips • Theatre and sports tickets • Recreation facilities • Reserved company parking • Work breaks • Sabbatical leaves • Club memberships and privileges • Discount purchase privileges • Personal loans at favorable rates • Free legal advice • Free personal financial planning advice • Free home protection-theft insurance • Burglar alarms and personal protection • Moving expenses • Home purchase assistance

3. **Status Symbols:** Office size and location • Office with window • Carpeting • Drapes • Paintings • Watches • Rings • Formal awards/recognition • Wall plaque

4. **Social Rewards:** Friendly greetings • Informal recognition • Praise • Smile • Evaluative feedback • Compliments • Nonverbal signals • Pat on the back • Invitations to coffee/lunch • After hours social gatherings

5. **Task Self-Rewards:** Interesting work • Sense of achievement • Job of more importance • Job variety • Job performance feedback • Self-recognition • Self-praise • Opportunity to schedule own work • Working hours • Participation in new organizational ventures • Choice of geographical location • Autonomy in job

Practices and Processes

Compensation Defined

Compensation is the sum of the direct and indirect monetary rewards paid to an employee for his/her contribution to the organization. In order to inspire people to maximize their efforts, compensation (policies, guidelines and processes) must be fair and perceived to be tied to organizational goals. In order to do so, most organizations adopt a formal process for determining rewards. This process is accomplished through 4 key activities:

- Job Design
- Job Description

- Job Evaluation
- Performance Evaluation/Appraisal

Job Designs are concerned with the content, functions, relationships and expected outcomes of jobs. Outcomes involve both task accomplishment (i.e. performance, productivity and so on) and human factors (i.e. satisfaction, turnover and absenteeism). Job design programs should consider both factors in development, implementation and evaluation. The most critical job design characteristics are skill variety, job significance, job identity, autonomy and feedback. *The 'design' should also clearly reflect the relationship between the job and the goals of the organization.*

EXERCISE

1. How does *coaching* fit into your job design?

_____

_____

_____

Job Descriptions specify the primary duties of people assigned to each job, as well as responsibilities and reporting relationships. *The 'description' should clearly reflect the relationship between the person in the job and the goals of the organization.*

EXERCISE

1. How is *coaching* described in your job?

_____

_____

_____

Job Evaluations compare jobs within an organization – their relative value (compensation/rewards), given the organizational goals. Evaluation is a 5-step process:

Step 1. Decide what the organization is paying for – determine which factors will be used to evaluate jobs. The factors used by organizations vary widely, but they all presumably reflect job-related contributions. Typically, organizations value jobs by measuring factors that describe accountability, complexity, inter-personal skill requirements, diversity, physical and mental demands.

Step 2. Choose a system for *evaluating jobs* – this requires selecting a system according to the factors chosen in Step 1. There are several methods of job evaluation: • the *ranking method* • the *job classification method* • the *point rating method* • the *factor-comparison* method:

- **Ranking Method** – Job 'analysis' (the result of job *design* and *descriptions*) is used to construct a hierarchy or ladder of jobs, which reflects their relative difficulty or value to the organization. One of the difficulties found with this method is that all jobs are forced to be different from each other. Often it's difficult to make fine distinctions between similar jobs and thus disagreements arise.
- **Job Classification Method** – This method is similar to the ranking method, except that classes or grades are established and the jobs are then placed into the classes. Jobs are usually evaluated on the basis of the whole job, often using one factor such as difficulty or an intuitive summary of factors. Again, job analysis information is useful in the classification, and benchmark jobs are frequently established for each class. Within each class or grade, there is no further ranking of the jobs.
- **Point Rating Method** – This method consists of assigning point values for previously determined factors and adding them to arrive at a total.
- **Factor-Comparison Method** – This method is similar to point rating in that both use factors. The point method uses degrees and points for each factor to measure jobs whereas the factor-comparison method uses benchmark jobs and relates money values to factors.

Step 3. Determine job grades – Once job evaluations are conducted, and before salaries are determined, using the results from a single job evaluation or several, job grades are created. Determining grades involves grouping all jobs that are similar in value such as all clerical or managerial jobs. Jobs within the same grade may be quite different, but they should be about equal or comparable in value to the organization. Each grade is assigned one salary or a range of salaries.

Step 4. Determine number of pay structures – It may be necessary to implement more than one 'pay' structure due to union or other considerations. Blue-collar positions may have a different pay structure than white. Technical positions may be graded differently than managerial. This is a decision that should be taken early on in the process.

Step 5. Design a pay structure – Job grades include guidelines for minimum and maximum levels of pay. The first step in the process is to develop a pay policy line (a trend line) that best represents the pay value of jobs. This line need not be straight, but it should portray the mid-point value of either benchmark jobs or all jobs that have been evaluated.

EXERCISE

1. What system of 'job evaluation' does your organization use?

_____

_____

_____

_____

2. How many 'job grades' does the organization have?

_____

_____

_____

_____

3. What should be the range for the minimum to the mid-point and maximum of a pay range?

_____

_____

_____

TIP

A 30% to 50% spread is popular but values above and below this range are quite common.

4. How much overlap should there be between grades?

_____

_____

_____

_____

TIP

A 10% difference in mid-points and 50% spread from minimum to maximum pay levels yields an 80% overlap per the following:

	Minimum	Mid-point	Maximum
Grade 1	$8,000	$10,000	$12,000
Grade 2	$8,800	$11,000	$13,200

5. Should there be steps within grades?

_____

_____

_____

_____

TIP

It's common to have an entry-level step, followed by a step after a standard probationary period, and then followed at regular intervals with steps that carry the employee through his/her progression in the job. A properly organized pay structure, competently administered and updated, will stimulate employee motivation and high levels of productivity.

EXERCISE

1. How is your job evaluated?

_____

_____

_____

_____

2. How would the coaching factors of 'credibility,' 'desire to,' 'skills' and 'capacity' fit into the process?

_____

_____

_____

_____

_____

_____

3. What values *should they have* in contributing to organizational goals?

_____

_____

_____

_____

_____

_____

Performance Evaluations/Appraisals – Job *descriptions* (responsibilities and duties) identify inputs to the work process. Job *evaluations* determine the worth of these inputs. Performance *evaluations* begin the movement toward identifying required outputs or outcomes by further describing processes required for carrying out a specific responsibility or duty. Performance *dimensions* identify the specific knowledge, skills, efforts and desires of the jobholder. Performance dimensions then integrate the unique qualities of the incumbent with the demands placed on the job. Critical performance dimensions are those components of job performance that are systematically determined to be the pivotal behaviors required for the successful accomplishment of the job.

The measuring of employee performance requires considerable information about relatively few things. It's for this reason that essential job requirements and distinctive features of an employee's job performance are grouped into rather small units for identification and observation purposes. Performance evaluations describe results in terms of quantity of output, quality of output, timeliness of output, effectiveness in use of resources, positive and negative effects of effort, manner of performance and method of performing assignments. Care must be taken to ensure that standards are stated in specific, understood terms that are attainable and valid.

In moving from job responsibilities (descriptions) to performance evaluations, it's possible to identify 15 to 20 goals. When this occurs, goals should be prioritized and only those that meet certain criteria should be used for appraisal purposes. Establishing performance goals ensures that all goal-directed work effort relates to the achievement of organizational goals, and that the goals of each individual and the work group are compatible with and supportive of results to be achieved by other organizational groups and units.

EXERCISE

1. How is your performance evaluated?

_____

_____

_____

2. How does *effective coaching* contribute to organizational goals?

_____

_____

_____

3. How can *effective coaching* be included in your performance evaluation process?

_____

_____

_____

Conclusion

By understanding how organizations define and evaluate supervisory positions and potential outcomes (performance), the manager/coach can present a stronger case to management for increasing personal rewards as the result of effective coaching.

Appendix

Coaching –
An Essence Debate

Appendix

INTRODUCTION

Business coaching was first recognized as an important management attribute in the late 1950s. General Electric unveiled the results of an internal study in which 90% of its top managers credited a prior boss as the most important factor to their success. This finding started a ground swell of interest in the concept of coaching – a concept that originates from the world of sports.

Drawing sports concepts into business is not new. The "winning is everything" attitude borrowed from two-time Super Bowl winning Coach Vince Lombardi is wide spread in today's business world. "Scoring," "wins and losses" and "team work" are examples of sports terms that are well entrenched in the '90s management jargon.

Today, corporations are constantly inviting winning coaches to speak at business functions about peak performance and about how to achieve it in a business setting. They are asked to describe what it takes to be a winner, how to set goals and work as a team and, how to motivate and be motivated.

The recent growth in popularity of "coaching" coincides with the increasing attention given to performance appraisal programs, mentoring programs, training programs and total quality management implementations. All of these activities require a measure of supervisor-subordinate interaction. They require some form of coaching.

At the outset there are two basic issues managers face that need to be addressed. One, there is no consensus on what business coaching really is and two, the causal relationship between coaching and corporate performance has not been proven, at least not empirically.

The purpose of this paper is to address these questions by first reviewing the debates that have promoted and challenged the essence of coaching. It examines the similarities and differences in the meanings given to "coaching" from three points of view: the management literature, the sport psychology literature and finally, personal interviews conducted with winning sport coaches and trainers.

The first section will review the evolution of coaching in management. It will summarize the positions taken by the various investigators of coaching. The second section will examine the coaching issues raised in sports – the root of coaching. The third section will present the results of personal interviews with successful sport coaches. The final section will summarize the information gathered and challenge the popular definition generally given to "coaching."

There are two subtle, yet distinctive streams to coaching; and Researchers are split into two Schools of Thought. First, those who believe that coaching is a "process," that is, a series of structured management activities that lead to improved team performance; or second, those who view coaching as a unique "management skill."

Business Coaching – The Literature

In 1971 Lovin and Casstevells were among the first investigators to describe coaching as a process – a process planned and performed by the manager for the purpose of developing his or her personnel. It includes evaluating people's skills in order to identify their strengths and weaknesses. It also includes determining together – both coach and subordinate – just what the subordinate needs in order to meet the requirements of the job. Finally, it includes follow-up to make sure the plan accomplishes it purposes. Singer (1974) also discusses coaching as a process or work activity to develop subordinates. He describes a good coach as someone "who is interested in his/her people, that looks for potential in people, that knows the interests, desires and capacities of subordinates." He goes on to say, "coaching is not just another technique of management development; rather it is the process by which the development of managers is achieved through continuous learning in their normal daily environment." Fournies (1979) describes coaching as a face-to-face process that helps managers more successfully bring about performance achievements in business that relate directly to the survival of that business.

Deegan (1983) describes a coach as "someone who is responsible for the development of people, on an on-going basis: planning the annual development of subordinates, giving on-the-job instructions, correcting mistakes when they occur, providing job rotation opportunities, providing time for development, developing replacement candidates, working with developmental resources (such as training departments), putting formal and informal developmental resources in place, planning upward career paths and identifying individuals with promotional potential. Peters & Austin (1985) describe effective coaching as a series of steps in improving understanding and performance through strong communication and motivation. Megginson & Boydell (1986) define coaching as a process in which managers, through direct discussion and guided activity, helps a colleague to learn to solve a problem, or do a task, better than would otherwise have been the case. Kinlaw (1989) describes coaching as a process by which managers stay in touch with their subordinates, that is "eyeball-to-eyeball" management. Chiaramonte (1993) views coaching as a cyclical process; once the coach has assessed the level of self-confidence and potential of an individual, he/she creates a vision of excellence and of what is possible. He/she secures a commitment from the performer and confronts fears and overcomes barriers. Finally, the coach establishes an evaluative process.

All of the above researchers favor the "process" approach as the better definition to coaching. They view it as a series of activities that are meshed together to enhance personal development.

Blake & Mouton, in 1964, were the first to describe the effective manager as a "superior communicator, a teacher and a coach – an important way for managers to engage individual employees sufficiently to build commitment to goals." They identified coaching as a skill separate from communications and teaching. They were among the first to view coaching as a unique management skill.

Mahler (1973) describes coaching as the ability to develop latent potential in subordinates. Atkinson (1980) describes the developmental responsibility of managers as "three distinct roles including coach, sponsor and mentor." Kirkpatrick (1982) summarizes coaching as "apt to take the form of working on forward-looking plans and objectives for subordinates in a way that keeps them moving constantly toward new areas of experience, new demands for personal skill development and application of ingenuity and problem solving. Day-to-day coaching takes place when the need arises. It bolsters the relationship between the manager and the subordinate." Orth, Wilkinson and Benfari (1987) discuss how organizations often do not provide a climate that rewards management coaching, there were few role models and managers had to work hard to change attitudes ... coaching was not a natural talent for most managers. Hein (1989) wrote a compelling thesis on coaching effectiveness in middle managers. He links effective coaching with effective teaching ... "the emphasis on elements such as feedback to the learner, a need to provide guidance to the learning process, encouragement of the learner and a need for clear learning goals permeates the literature on teaching as it pertains to coaching."

In spite of the volume of research discussing 'coaching,' there has not been extensive empirical research done to evaluate the causal relationship between business coaching and corporate performances (profitability or productivity). The sense is that, intuitively at least, coaching is important to individual and group performances, and is largely based on a set of skills and processes that logically lead to good communication and presumably good relations between a supervisor and his/her subordinates. The reality, however, is that the business world is left with a fashionable new concept in "coaching" but had yet to really prove its worth. No one has demonstrated the value of coaching and its contribution to the performance outcome of an organization.

In the next section, the paper will examine the origin of coaching. It will describe the evolution of coaching in sport, the paradigms within sport and explain its leap into business today.

Sport Coaching – The Literature

Sport coaching goes back to Ancient Greece (Gusdorf, 1967) and the first sports trainers. Rauch (1982) describes the first coaches as "trainers." The trainer was responsible for the physical conditioning of the athlete by managing biological needs in order to meet specific physical performance objectives. Two thousand years later, in the mid XIXth century, a more scientific approach to training was introduced – a biochemical approach. Food could be measured in terms of energy inputs or calories – an important discovery in terms of contribution to an athlete's performance. In order to improve the preparation of individual athletes, the effective coach needed to understand this new science. It wasn't until the early XXth century that sport psychology was recognized as an equally important science in terms of understanding athletic performances. An effective coach now needed to understand not only the physical inputs for high-performance athletes but also mental inputs. In North America, psychologist Coleman R. Griffith is recognized as the father of sport psychology (LeUnes & Nation, 1989; Williams & Straub, 1993). He was the first to research sport psychology over an extended period of time. He established the first sport laboratory at the University of Illinois in 1925.

The sport literature generally views "coaching" as a function independent of that of the "Manager." The "Coach" is responsible for managing the players of the team once the "General Manager" has recruited them. Unlike some of the management literature in which coaching is one of several functions performed by a manager. In sport, coaching and managing are usually two separate jobs. Coaching is usually linked with team performance while "managing" is usually tied to team administration. One thing is clear, however, in sport and especially professional sports, if the athlete or team does not win, the coach is often the first person to be removed (fired). The coach is a key figure in the success of a team and investigators have taken a quantitative approach to proving it. The conclusion is that the role and value of "coaching" in sports is unequivocal: coaching is a determining factor in team performance. The debate, however, is on the "how" to be an effective coach.

There are literally hundreds of sport psychology studies investigating the concept of coaching. Over the years, sport adopted many popular management theories and fit them into a sports context. For example, Sage (1974) discusses the similarities between coaching athletes and managing employees and the evolution from a Machiavellian management style to a humanistic approach. Referring to researchers like Mayo (1933), Lewin (1935), McGregor (1960) and Maslow (1965), it was clear that athletic coaches needed to change their ways and be more in keeping with contemporary management values and ethics that emphasize individuality and freedom from capricious autocratic control. Today the task of the athletic coach is to enhance the player's potential and achieve self-fulfillment. And this is not unlike the task being proposed for business managers. In the last 25 years, sport researchers have focused extensively on "how" to be an effective coach. A large body of the research was oriented towards "leadership" and "decision making" models developed from organizational psychology. Murray & Mann (1993) discuss the varied interpretations of effective coaching and leadership qualities. Research on leadership has attempted to identify personal qualities and behaviours that are most likely to result in leader effectiveness and to determine what influence, if any, specific situational factors have on these variables. Such research has resulted in testing trait, behavioral, situational and transformational approaches to leadership theory. These investigators summarize that being a good coach involves an appreciation of leadership theory and knowledge of how a coach can maximize the influence on followers through positive role modeling, planning, preparation and being true to oneself. With insight, knowledge and sensitivity toward individual differences, all coaches can be successful.

There is, however, no consensus on what an "effective" coach is supposed to do all the time. Studies contradict one another. For example, in Fielder's Contingency Model of Leadership (1967) that characterizes leaders as either task-oriented and autocratic or interpersonally-oriented and democratic, researchers have come to different conclusions. Danielson (1976) found that the most effective coaching was person-oriented rather than task-oriented. Bird (1977) found that winning coaches in the more highly skilled sports programs were people-oriented while the opposite was true in a less-skilled program. Chelladurai (1993) concludes that an autocratic decision style is quite acceptable in certain circumstances and that a coach needs to select a style appropriate to the situation rather than being guided by the belief that participative decisions are always superior or preferred. There is the Path-Goal Theory of Leadership (House, 1971,1974) that suggests that the coach's function is to provide

Appendix

a "path" guidance, support and rewards necessary for effective performance (House, 1971). It too is inconclusive (Carron, 1987; Chelladurai & Carron, 1978; Chelladurai & Salesh, 1978; Von Strache, 1979).

Murray & Mann (1993) state that there is some evidence to support the concept that successful coaches possess certain dispositions that appear constant, consistent and immutable over time and across situations. These dispositions are anxiety levels, friendliness and eagerness for novel experiences. Paying attention to their appearance, demonstrating self-confidence and expertise, appropriately allocating rewards and sanctions and being an example to admire and emulate are ways in which coaches can increase their potential influence. LeUnes & Nation (1993) describe the majority of coaches as being aware that coaching is more than "Xs and Os" – it underscores the importance to properly motivating athletes to do their best. Coaching is nothing more than teaching; the coach should be knowledgeable about the activity being taught. Athletes need to be taught the basic skills or fundamentals that are essential to excellent performance. Coaches who are methodical and orderly in the teaching of skills and who are expert in the proper application of positive reinforcement and punishment (with emphasis on reinforcement) are miles ahead of their lesser informed contemporaries .... The successful coach is a motivator. The good coach will be forceful but democratic, allowing for considerable individual input into the everyday management of the sport at hand, whether team or individual. At times the coach must become a disciplinarian ... he clearly states the code of player conduct up front and adheres to it with reasonable regularity ... if punishment is to be successful in changing behavior, it must be mild, prompt and consistent. The good coach leads by example ... a coach who demands hard work is also a hard worker ... the coach who commands respect should show respect for others.

In sport, the coach is viewed very differently than in management. Yager (1993) points out that contrary to business, an athletic coach's role is tied to outcomes and not administration. In sports, the coach focuses on performance and results, on both individual and team growth. Goals are more important in sports, they are clear, simple and constant ... the coach must WIN. Great coaches measure outputs that drive outcome. In sports, rewards are tied to achievements not to effort.

The general approach to coaching in sport is clearly more scientific. Researchers rely on constructs from the fields of psychology and sociology to prove their points. In sport, there is little debate as to whether coaching is essential to team performance. Save for the few that argue that the superstars don't need a coach, this has yet to be proven empirically.

Sport Coaching – The Interviews

In order to support the conclusions derived from the sport literature, a series of interviews were conducted with coaches and trainers to get a present-day view of the coach-performance relationship. The next section will look at the results of interviews with four of the most successful professional sport coaches and/or their trainers in the 90s.

Few people understand the full role of trainers on a team. But once understood, their contribution to this research is extremely important, in fact essential. First, trainers/therapists are very reliable informants for the purpose of this paper. For research purposes they are able to observe the coach every day, under several working conditions (game situations, practice sessions, clubhouse environment). Over the course of their careers, sports therapists will work under many coaches. This gives them a comparative base to evaluate different coaching behaviours and outcomes. The four sports therapists/trainers interviewed for this paper have observed on a full-time basis the behaviours and performances of 26 professional sports coaches. Each sports therapist spends on average five hours per game-day within seeing or hearing distance of the head coach. Another important reason for interviewing the sports therapists is that they interact with players on a daily basis to treat sports injuries and supervise rehabilitation programs. After the coach, they are the ones who interact with players the most. As a result, they build a strong rapport with the players. They hear about players' concerns and their relationship with the coach. They get the players' perceptions of the coach's behaviours. Because of these reasons and their availability and willingness to be interviewed, sports therapists' insights into effective coaching behaviours are quite pertinent.

The Interviews:

#1 What's an effective coach?

Felipe Alou: "The coach must be prepared for the job ... know the trade well so there is no question among the players about the coach knowing the trade."

Expos (Trainer): "Recognises the talent he's working with ... utilizes that talent in a proper way ... is a good communicator."

Jacques Demers: "A coach who puts in a system that everyone believes in ... be extremely honest and forward with your players ... to organise good practices ... to communicate with your players."

Canadiens Trainer: "Brings 20-25 different individuals into becoming 1 unit, a team ... able to listen ... he's friend but also somebody you can't really push because you don't know where the limit lies."

Bills (Trainer): "Improves the players' self esteem ... instils confidence ... knows how to control egos ... knows when to chastise a team and when not to ... doesn't try to do everything himself ... has enough confidence in the guys they have and let them do it ... has everyone working towards a common goal ... is a great psychologist ... treats every player individually ... is a good delegator."

Blue Jays (Trainer): "Has to communicate ... talk on a daily basis ... at least have an open door policy ... gets the most out of his players ... the players play for him ... knows when to give them days off, to stroke them, when not to ... has just enough presence not to get overrun yet he maintains a certain amount of pressure on them all the time."

#2 What are the responsibilities of a coach?

Felipe Alou: "To keep the team together … to focus … to improve the quality of the game, the production. And to detect if there is any lack of production or a decrease in production – not only team wise but also individually. The coach needs to have a tremendous amount of honesty and a sense of responsibility towards the group…"

Expos (Trainer): "Delegates responsibilities to the coaching staff … delegates authority … works with his personnel … puts right player in right position … able to answer questions … shows good work habits … sets example."

Jacque Demers: "To emphasise the importance of team concept, the role of each player on the team … a coach should communicate with the players. The responsibility of the coach is always to think team, to make sure that if there is a problem to deal with that problem."

Canadiens (Trainer): "Varies with the type of team … .Playing in Montreal is an every day thing – 12 months of the year … the players react differently … coaching the Montreal Canadiens is bigger than life … allow closeness but not too close … gets the best out of me every day."

Bills (Trainer): "Keeps in mind the good of the team … controls what they're supposed to do … teaches the players self-discipline."

Blue Jays (Trainer): "Teaches or instructs … directs and instils every day living … the good things about life."

#3   Why do you meet with players individually and as a group?

Felipe Alou: "Obviously when it's a team meeting it has to do with the welfare of the group. It has to do with the direction the group is going or the lack of direction. It might be the problem of one player but it needs to be addressed as a team problem because sometimes a one-player problem can affect the team … be careful not to humiliate a member of the team in front of the other players."

Expos (Trainer): "Depends on the group and the player … once you know your personnel, the coach steps in whenever they waver off course … depends on the situation, attitude of the player."

Jacques Demers: "You need to meet with players [individually] before the season starts. Last year we won the cup and this year we weren't as successful, so at the end of the season I met with the players to find out the reasons why. A coach needs to know what his players are thinking and the players need to know what the coaches are thinking. It's extremely important to communicate with them, to be honest with them, to be forward in your talk … not to sidestep questions when a player needs to know … you need to tell him directly to his face. Group meetings are very important … not to over do it … there should be meetings during the regular season … too many group meetings tend to lose the players … they get fed up. You should have them but not too many of them. At the end of the season, before the playoffs start you should have a good meeting with each player, redefining their role and letting them know what they have to do in that specific series."

Canadiens (Trainer): "Individually, they'll meet during the post-season to make an evaluation … has an open-door policy … you can see him without scheduling a meeting any time you need to. There are team meetings before every game … but that's tactical. He's truly honest … not phoney."

Bills (Trainer): "To give attention to certain players who need pepping up or have a problem … to criticize as opposed to chastising on the field … will give praise on the field but won't be hyper-critical of a player."

Blue Jays (Trainer): "Individually for private reasons … to discuss a negative issue … for disciplinary reasons … as a group, to encourage someone or discuss an issue, or maybe to single out a particular player for positive reasons and recognition … make a positive statement about a guy who did something well."

#4   What resources/assets do you need to be a successful coach? Why?

Felipe Alou: "I need the other coaches … my firm belief is that no one person alone can manage a team. It's impossible. Nobody is that energetic; nobody is that smart to handle a team alone. You need to delegate … we have professional people with talent handling very important responsibilities in this group."

Expos (Trainer): "Has good communication skills … explains what he wants them to do … needs a firm handle on the team as well as on the individual … has to know his business … experience really helps … have built-in respect for what they have done in the past … have one set of rules but be flexible … get the best out of your team, that's success."

Jacques Demers: "The coach has to be a proven winner. If you never win you don't get the respect of your players. You can't demand respect … respect comes from winning … I think it's extremely important to have won and to have instant credibility with your players at that level. The players must know that when the coach comes in he's in charge. The players need a leader, they need to know that the coach is well organized and knows what he's talking about."

Canadiens (Trainer): "Needs to be flexible ... able to communicate ... lives up to his commitments ... pays tribute to those who deserve it."

Bills (Trainer): "Good and smart players ... good environment to work in ... good locker room facilities ... travel in first class manner."

Blue Jays (Trainer): "Utilizes the staff, delegates different jobs ... gets information from the staff ... utilizes everything ... gets different opinions and views, compiles them all and derives a conclusion."

#5   How do you increase, maintain, reward a player's performance?

Felipe Alou: "And you also have to reward people with good words, encouraging words like "nice going" when the player is doing well and encouraging words when they are not doing so well. I really don't do it every day because I don't think they will appreciate it, because we work every day. This is not the five-day workweek and then everybody goes home for the weekend. We work seven days a week. We have to be careful here not to become too bothersome to the people that are here. My behaviour towards players has always been to keep a comfortable distance, respectful distance ... to be friendly with the player, but they cannot touch me with their hand, they are not close enough to touch me with their hand. But they are not too far away if they need to find me and talk to me. I keep my door open.

I know there are times just by the look ... you look at a player and he knows. For example you tell a player "nice going" just by the look. We have to be careful how we look at the people that are under us. We have to show understanding, love, appreciation and encouragement ... by the look we give. It doesn't have to be words ... otherwise I believe they will find it kind of phoney. Because of all the personal contact we have here ... in aeroplanes, hotel lobbies, meetings, ball games, buses, clinics, hospitals ... it's almost like a family for all of the months we're together. We create a little bit of a space between the players and coaches and players and the manager to make sure that we don't get to sticky to the player and vice versa. Because I know there was a situation here before where it became almost like a minor league kind of operation. Once a man gets up to this level and plays couple of years, you're dealing with a major league character, we have to be careful because they become very independent. They put a lot of money in their pockets ... but money is not the most important thing ... we still keep a good relationship with them. But we keep a little bit of space to make sure that we don't get too close to them."

Expos (Trainer): "Knowing the team, the players, knowing what they need ... some guys need a pat on the back, pampered and coddled while others need a kick in the butt ... no two players are the same."

Jacques Demers: "You need to upgrade his ice time; he needs to be told at times face to face; earlier in the year you may have brought in that player and said you weren't happy with his performance and as soon as you upgrade his performance you need to bring him into your office and tell him that, at one given time I wasn't pleased with your performance, but now your performance level is up, your playing a lot better. The way I'm now thinking is that you can contribute to the team's success. And I think that's the key."

Canadiens (Trainer): "There is no pre-set pattern. You have to go back to the individual. Some need to be talked to a lot; they'll perform well if they feel the coach is more concerned about the individual than the player. For some other guy, no matter what you say, it's a job – they're going to work. What's interesting is the fact that more players are coming from single-parent homes and the coach has to take part of the dad's job. Life in the 90s is different; you have to be sensitive to what's underneath the sweater. If a guy is sending you a yellow light that means he's in trouble and needs someone to help him; a broken heart takes a lot more time to heal than a ripped knee. In the 90s, you have to make that adjustment."

Bills (Trainer): "Praises him in front of his peers ... would wait until the team had a good game and everyone had a good feeling about themselves and they would mention negative that happened two weeks earlier – when they could take it ... if the team won he would be very critical and when they lose he was their best friend."

Blue Jays (Trainer): "With a positive statement and a handshake every time, no matter how small ... give him a pat on the back to make a positive statement ... not afraid to put a player who has failed back into the line-up ... encourages the player ... gets the player to continue to practice and to work ... sticks by his promise ... always backs up what he says."

#6   When would you adopt a democratic management style?

Felipe Alou: "Yes, there are times when the club is not winning, we are falling short, the team is making mistakes. Over the long year, mistakes are going to be made by me, by a coach, by a player, by the team. So [when this happens] I find it is time to get a little closer to the group and get the coaches involved. Get myself involved. Sometimes we discuss openly with the players, everybody to hear what they have to say. Because they have some things they want to share ... with us concerning winning ball games. Sometimes I'll bring in the hitting coach and ask him if I should change the line-up or if there is a batter I should walk today...because I feel like I'm failing the way I'm doing. Sometimes I'll bring in all of the coaches here ... because there are times of crisis like any other group. And there are times that you may not be going through a crisis but you could see it coming. You have to be able to anticipate. It's the obligation of the coach and the staff to be ahead of the storm. So when the storm hits, you will be fully prepared...and you won't be hurt as badly. This is a very important part of this business.

Just like it is for a player. We can see when a player is starting to hit into a slump or the pitcher is starting to dip his elbow, that the pitching coach has to address the problem. He tries to straighten the player out before he walks five guys and gets pulled from the ball game or loses four or five games. We are very conscious here because of the kind of environment, operation and budget we have to work with. We have to be on top of everything, big and small. In fact we don't have too many big things to address because we make sure to address the problems when they are very small. When we get a "storm" we let it hit us when it's not powerful; we don't let a storm really develop. And that's a critical factor in all kinds of business. You can't be surprised by the negative. You have to be on top. Otherwise you're not doing your job."

Expos (Trainer): "Never ... only one man in charge ... he might get opinions."

Jacques Demers: "I think my communication with my General Manager is the key to my success. I think the GM needs to know what is the situation of player changes: why certain players are not in the line-up ... why you made line changes. The GM usually doesn't want to coach but he needs to be aware ... he's your boss ... needs to know what you're thinking. Once he knows that there's tremendous communication and once the players know that the GM and coach are strong together and work together, it's a difficult barrier to cross. The assistant coaches need to understand their role, need to have a freedom of speech with the players to feel comfortable that they can talk with the players. I think it's very important that a coach is not looking over his shoulder (at assistant coaches) is not an insecure coach. It's a very insecure job ... and I think there are a lot of insecure coaches in our profession. I think if a coach feels ... according to my eleven years in NHL ... the coach feels secured. A lot of times when coaches are not financially set they are always looking over their shoulders because maybe people want their job. In my case it's not. I feel comfortable giving full freedom to my assistant coaches and not worry about telling them anything. And I encourage them to express their views as to what we need to do to become a successful team."

Canadiens (Trainer): "Has an open door policy ... if there's a specific project, I'm sure he consults different players, the captain and the senior players."

Bills (Trainer): "Doesn't ... can let his coaches have some say about which plays to run."

Blue Jays (Trainer): "Listens for the players' needs and keeps an open line of communication ... military and strict rules do not work in today's society with today's players ... he lets the players play ... takes in information ... treats players like he wanted to be treated when he was playing."

The Characteristics

From the 3 primary sources of origin, 61 characteristics describing effective coaching were extracted. The characteristics cover a range of personal attributes that describe the profile of successful coaches and their environment. For example, the attitudes, skills and behaviours generally regarded as being essential to effective coaching were extracted. Other examples are the 'types' of resources that are required to be effective. And finally, other personal attributes that were mentioned several times, like respect and honesty were also extracted.

   To better examine the information, the 61 characteristics were consolidated into 38 characteristics (later pared down to 33) and sorted according to their source of origin and frequency of use (See Tables 1, 2, 3, 4). For example, the characteristic "Individual Attention given by the coach" is reported 5 times in the Sport Psychology Literature, 3 times in the Management Literature and 7 times in the Personal Interviews with successful sports coaches. What this means is that this characteristic is the most often cited characteristic among all the characteristics extracted, that is, 15 times among all sources.

Appendix

Table 1: Characteristics taken from the 3 sources and sorted by 'Total' Frequency

	Characteristics	Source: Sport Psychology Literature	Source: Management Literature	Source: Personal Interviews	Total
1	Individual Attention	5	3	7	15
2	Motivator	1	6	5	12
3	Consultative/Democratic	2	4	5	11
4	Evaluation/Feedback	1	9	1	11
5	Teacher	2	5	4	11
6	Team Focus	2	2	7	11
7	Communication	1	5	4	10
8	Delegation	0	4	5	9
9	Respect	1	3	5	9
10	Flexibility	2	3	3	8
11	Listener	1	4	2	7
12	Personal Development	0	7	0	7
13	Reinforcement	0	4	3	7
14	Technical Excellence	3	2	2	7
15	Credibility	1	1	4	6
16	People-oriented	2	2	2	6
17	Role Model	3	2	1	6
18	Sets Goals	1	5	0	6
19	Honest	0	2	3	5
20	Dedication	0	1	3	4
21	Firm	1	0	3	4
22	Follow-up	0	3	1	4
23	Leader	2	1	1	4
24	Practice	0	1	3	4
25	Prepared	2	0	2	4
26	Relates to All	2	2	0	4
27	Sensitive	3	0	1	4
28	Availability	0	2	2	4
29	Timing	0	3	1	4
30	Meet Control Needs	1	0	2	3
31	Non-verbal	1	0	2	3
32	Rewarding	1	2	0	3
33	Disciplinarian	2	0	1	3
34	Talent	0	0	3	3
35	Strong	1	2	0	3
36	Meet Social Needs	2	0	0	2
37	Time	0	2	0	2
38	Strategic	0	0	2	2

Table 2: Top 14 Characteristics taken from the **Sport Psychology Literature** and sorted by Frequency

Characteristics	Frequency
Individual Attention	5
Role Model	3
Sensitive	3
Technical Excellence	3
Consultative/Democratic	2
Disciplinarian	2
Flexibility	2
Leader	2
Meet Social Needs	2
People-oriented	2
Prepared	2
Relates to All	2
Teacher	2
Team Focus	2

Table 3: Top 15 Characteristics taken from the **Management Literature** and sorted by Frequency

Characteristics	Frequency
Evaluation/Feedback	9
Personal Development	7
Motivator	6
Communication	5
Sets Goals	5
Teacher	5
Consultative/Democratic	4
Delegation	4
Listener	4
Reinforcement	4
Flexibility	3
Follow-up	3
Individual Attention	3
Respect	3
Timing	3

Appendix

Table 4: Top 16 Characteristics taken from the **Personal Interviews** and sorted by Frequency

Characteristics	Frequency
Individual Attention	7
Team Focus	7
Consultative/Democratic	5
Delegation	5
Motivator	5
Respect	5
Communication	4
Credibility	4
Teacher	4
Dedication	3
Firm	3
Flexibility	3
Honest	3
Practice	3
Reinforcement	3
Talent	3

The next step was to separate the characteristics into homogeneous groups. Without any specific regard for the order in which they are ranked, groups of characteristics were formed according to similarities in their nature and/or function. For example, characteristics like "respect," "honesty" and CREDIBILITY belong together because of their direct rapport with an individual's "being" or personality traits. They reflect individual traits that are related to repeated accomplishments and generally earned only after an extended period of time. Another group was formed around a person's ability to "do" things; for example, "teaching," "communicating," "listening," "organizing" and "delegating" seem to belong together and so on.

From this distilling process, four groups eventually evolved. In order to explain the essence of each group, a descriptive label called "principal factor" was assigned to each group. The four principal factors that emerged and best explained the essence of each group are Credibility, Desire, Skills and Slack, respectively.

The next section examines the principal factors and the characteristics that make them up.

PRINCIPAL FACTORS OF EFFECTIVE COACHING

The CREDIBILITY factor is made up of the characteristics that relate to "a subordinate's confidence level in the supervisor/coach." For example, a subordinate's perception of the supervisor's "technical competence" will impact on the subordinate's confidence level in the supervisor. The full list of characteristics that were extracted and related to a "a subordinate's confidence level in the supervisor/coach," in other words, the supervisor's credibility, are:

Respect: The esteem a subordinate has for a supervisor

Dedication: A supervisor's demonstrated commitment to a cause; " the supervisor works harder than anyone else in the group."

Honesty: A supervisor's straightforwardness and adherence to the facts.

Role Modeling: The supervisor is an example of conduct for the subordinates.

Technical Competence: The supervisor has an understanding of the technical issues that is beyond reproach.

Team-focused/strategic: Being team-oriented; that is, activities and decisions made by the supervisor are always made in the best interest of the group, as opposed to an individual member of the group; in the end, the team plays, wins and losses as a group. Day-to-day decisions made by the supervisor are consistent with pre-set objectives and plans – all decisions are made with the same, one objective in mind – to hit a specific target (win an event, or attain a specific level of competence) … the greater the consistency, the greater the credibility.

Leadership: The state of effectively directing a group of individuals towards a specified goal.

Values: Morally responsible – recognized as a "good" person.

Credibility: Believability.

Of the 60 references to characteristics that make up CREDIBILITY, 50% of them come from one primary source, the Interviews. By adding the references in the Management Literature by one author, Kirkpatrick (1982), whose findings are based on a survey of successful sports coaches, the number of references to CREDIBILITY jumps to 60%. This is significant in that the references are not proportionally distributed among the 3 sources under study. A range of 30%-40% is expected – not 60%. Given the high number of references from the "Interviews" source, coaches clearly recognize CREDIBILITY to be a more important factor than does either the Sport or Management Literatures. Of the 228 total references recorded, CREDIBILITY accounts for 24% of all the references.

In summary, the 9 characteristics that make up the CREDIBILITY factor are Respect, Honesty, Technical Competence, Dedication, being a Role Model, being a Leader, being Team-focused/Strategic, being Morally Responsible and Believable.

The second principal factor, DESIRE, is defined as " the manager's willingness to … (undertake specific coaching tasks)." For example, "If necessary, is the coach willing to be firm" or give regular "individual attention?" The full list of characteristics or tasks that make up this factor are:

Discipline: To correct or penalize for improper conduct.
Firm: To be steadfast on proper conduct.
Individual Attention: To provide specific attention to each subordinate.
Flexibility: To respond to a changing situation.
Evaluation/Feedback: To assess and comment an individual's performance.
Personal Development: To explore an employee's career track.
People-oriented: To enjoy social interaction and is sensitive to other people's needs.

Three of the four most often cited characteristics of effective coaching are grouped under the factor DESIRE (See Table 1): "Individual Attention," "Motivator" and "Evaluation/Feedback." The Management Literature puts an especially large emphasis on "Evaluations/Feedback" as important determinants to effective coaching. Almost 90% of all references to this characteristic emanate from the Management Literature.

There is one characteristic that investigators recognized as being critical and yet not often mentioned; and that is "Rewards." Clearly, the reward system associated with coaching must be equitable in order to attract and retain effective coaches. The coach could – in the form of money, time or other benefits – deem compensation important. As discussed later in the paper, the availability of other resources that come under SLACK will impact on the DESIRE to coach.

In summary, the 7 characteristics that make up the DESIRE factor are the supervisor's willingness to Discipline, be Firm, provide Individual Attention, be Flexible, provide Evaluation/Feedback, be interested in the Personal Development of a subordinate and finally be People-oriented. An equitable reward system is also an essential element of this factor.

The third principal factor, SKILL, is defined as "the aptitude to successfully complete an activity, alone and with others." The factor is divided into two sub-groups: People Skills and Task Skills. For example, "People Skills" include the ability to provide "contingent reinforcement," to "communicate" and "listen" to others. "Task Skills" include "organization" as well as abilities to "set goals," "delegate" and have effective "practices." The full lists of characteristics that make up this factor are:

a) People Skills:
Communication: Ability to send the information intended.
Teaching: Ability to instruct.
Listening: Ability to receive the information intended.
Relate to all: Ability to establish and maintain rapport with all the members of a group.
Consultative: Ability to consult with members of a group before making a decision.
Contingent Reinforcement: Ability to provide effective feedback following a specific outcome.

b) Task Skills:
Goal setting: Ability to identify challenging and reasonable individual and group goals.
Organization: Ability to prioritize and co-ordinate activities for the purpose of attaining a specific goal.
Preparation: Ability to gather beforehand and understand pertinent information.
Practice: Ability to plan and execute effective training sessions.
Delegation: Ability to strategically spread the workload among subordinates.
Follow-up: Ability to observe and intervene in post-training results.

The characteristics supporting "People SKILLS" appear to be proportionally distributed among the three primary sources. "Teaching," "Communications," "Listening" and "Contingent Reinforcement" represent about 16% of the total references. While the Management Literature leaves no doubt to the importance of "Setting Goals" for effective coaching, none of the coaches interviewed mentioned it as an important characteristic.

There are four characteristics that stand out, not because of the number of times they were mentioned in the sources, but because of the emphasis given to them by the researchers and interviewees. They are "Teaching," "Practice," "Non-verbal" and "Delegation."

"Teaching" underscores the point that an effective supervisor /coach be constantly alert to opportunities to transfer knowledge or instruct a subordinate on performance matters. For example, if an employee is having a problem with a specific process, the coach will intervene by first evaluating the situation and instruct the right approach in a clear and positive manner.

"Practice" is a concept that is more widely used in sports than in business. The interesting aspect, however, is that in

235

Appendix

management as in sport, the greater the quantity and quality a skill is practiced the better its execution in the field; execution of the skill becomes automatic and the doubt that often creeps into the user's consciousness is removed. The more a skill is practiced, the greater the self-confidence a user acquires in applying it in a real situation.

"Delegation" is an underrated "Task Skill." It requires special mention because of the extraordinary importance given to it in the Literatures and interviews. The interviewees, especially, are unequivocal on this point – "the ability to delegate tasks and responsibilities to subordinates" is among the most important characteristics of successful coaches. Typically, because of the range of responsibilities and subsequent tasks a coach undertakes, it is not unusual for the coach to be simply overwhelmed by the events. Unless he/she shares (delegates) the workload, failure to reach the goals is imminent.

The Interviews revealed three critical "sub-skills" or "personality attributes" not mentioned in any of the other primary sources. They are retained for two reasons: one, the interviewed coaches placed a great amount of emphasis as to their importance; and second, their acquisition becomes an integral component of any future training program involving skills related to these sub-skills and attributes.

The first sub-skill is "anticipation." It is the ability to look ahead and avoid surprises. This sub-skill is related to "organization" skills because it represents an ability to plan and forecast probable events that could negatively impact on performance. A strong sense of anticipation minimizes potential disasters and maximizes favorable opportunities.

An important attribute associated with successful coaches is their need for "perfection." Perfection is associated with a coach's extreme desire to "practice" perfectly so that in the field a skill is performed automatically and flawlessly. This emphasizes the need for greater quantity and quality of training sessions, especially practical application exercises where an individual is required to execute a learned skill repeatedly. The result is a skill being executed competently every time.

Finally, the "Look," as Felipe Alou calls it, is the last sub-skill emphasized. It is another effective method of "communicating." The supervisor communicates his/her viewpoint with their eyes only. This sub-skill is especially effective in situations relating to issues that don't require any further explanation. For example, improper conduct by a subordinate within a group setting might require only a "look" by the supervisor. In these situations, it is expected that everyone, especially the targeted subordinate, readily understand the supervisor's mute message; that is, " the conduct is inappropriate." This type of feedback is very effective when there is no need for a long and verbose reprimand. A "look" by the coach is also effective and sufficient in very positive situations where an individual meets and exceeds expectations on an on-going basis. Words of praise and appreciation can be substituted with a "look," or other non-verbal gestures like a handshake or a "thumbs-up."

In summary, the 12 characteristics that make up the SKILLS factor are the abilities to Communicate, Teach, Listen, Relate to Others, Consult, provide Contingent Reinforcement, to Set Goals, Organize, Prepare, Practice, Delegate and Follow-up. The sub-skills and attributes of "anticipation", "perfection" and "look" must also be regarded as essential characteristics of SKILLS.

The fourth and final principal factor, SLACK, is defined as "the availability and deployment of resources." "Time," "money," "information" and "equipment" are components of SLACK that are essential to the successful completion of an activity. It is a relatively new management term that represents "freedom of constraints" – constraints that usually bind and confine an organization and its people from acting in a given situation. Some call it excess capacity or, having a little more resource than what is exactly and usually required. It is emerging as an important strategic management concept for guiding organizations in the 1990s. It is seen as a critical element of innovation.

SLACK is made up of environmental attributes that were mentioned in the Literatures or Interviews. They include Talent, Time, Support, Money, Information and Equipment.

"Talent" is defined as an effective pool of human resources. Felipe Alou echoes the claims of many other coaches when he says "the most important factor to being successful is an effective recruiting process" that ensures a strong "talent" base. This suggests that "recruiting" skills be included in "Task Skills" as an additional critical skill to effective coaching.

Other attributes include:

> Time: an irrecoverable resource.
> Support: the assistance of superiors, colleagues and subordinates.
> Money: a financial resource/critical element of the reward system.
> Information: a strategic input for decision-making.
> Equipment: a material resource.

Each one of the above attributes is essential to a successful coaching program. Without them the program fails. How often do we hear: "I don't have the time, money, or equipment to do the job right" or "I'm not getting the support from above" or "If people don't tell me what's going on, how can I instruct my people?" Clearly, the quantity and quality of resources available and deployed in organizations are core elements of effective coaching programs.

Finally, "Space" is a unique SLACK characteristic of sport coaching that is not part of the group of characteristics listed in Tables 1-4. Yet, it warrants investigation because of its obvious impact on performance. It is described as the physical distance between a player and his/her coach. In sport, the physical closeness during an event is critical. The coach provides on-the-job direction and feedback. It's traditional and accepted as part of the event. In a management setting, post-training follow up could benefit from a similar environment in which supervisors spend more time in closer proximity with their subordinates.

The next section will examine the weighting given to each principal factor within and between each source of origin – Sport Psychology Literature, Management Literature and Interviews with coaches.

Summary of Principal Factors

The principal factors are not given the same degree of importance between the three primary sources of origin. This was dis-

236

covered by selecting the "top" 14 characteristics listed under Sport Psychology Literature, the "top" 15 characteristics under Management Literature and the "top" 16 characteristics under Interviews (the break point was established at the closest frequency change). Then, by assigning a score to each factor according to the number of characteristics that fell within its grouping and were stated among the "top" characteristics in each column. For example, with respect to the Sport Psychology Literature source, the factor DESIRE has a score of 4 (See Table 2.). What this means is that there are 4 characteristics in Table 2 that belong to the factor DESIRE.

Table 5

Source	DESIRE	SKILLS	CREDIBILITY	SLACK	OTHER
Sports Psych.	4	5	3	0	2
Management	5	8	1	1	0
Interviews	4	6	5	1	0

Table 5 presents the overall weighting differences. In summary, the Sport Psychology Literature leans towards SKILLS (score of 5) as the principal factors for effective coaching. It also recognizes DESIRE (score of 4) and CREDIBILITY (score of 3) as important factors. The Management Literature clearly views SKILLS (score of 8) as the critical factor leading to effective coaching with some recognition to DESIRE (score of 5) as a critical factor. It completely discounts the CREDIBILITY factor. Finally, the Interviews with sport coaches indicate an even distribution of the factors, with a slight favouring for SKILLS and CREDIBILITY.

What Does It Mean

The focus for learning and applying effective coaching behaviours is not consistent between the primary sources. It means that CREDIBILITY is virtually ignored by the Management Literature. It also means that certain skill sets have been seriously underrated in the popular management literature. Finally it means that a review of critical coaching characteristics is needed.

Effective coaching is more than an act of "Doing" something. It is more than just having strong communication skills, or the ability to organize, set goals and follow-up. Of course these skills and others are essential to effective coaching but by themselves are not enough to ensure effective coaching. For example, being CREDIBLE is not something a person "does" – it is not a skill. It is something a person IS. An effective coach is someone who is respected, honest, dedicated and a role model for others. It is someone, who has personal values, is "team-oriented" and is perceived as a leader. CREDIBILITY is one of the "Being" factors and is earned over a period of time and events. It cannot be learned like a skill.

The DESIRE to coach is the other "Being" factor. It cannot be taught. The desire to work with people, provide individual attention, be firm, be flexible and be disciplined are something a person "is." This trait is either internally driven or promoted through incentives. As mentioned earlier, an equitable "reward" system could reinforce someone's desire to want to coach.

"Doing" skills, however, remain key elements to an effective coaching program. SKILLS can be learned, taught and evaluated. Unless the problem is one of motivation, performance gaps can generally be redressed through pertinent skill-based training. For example, communication and organization skills can be taught. So, unlike the other factors, a training program can effectively overcome performance deficiencies, providing the individual is motivated to do so.

SLACK is the "Have" factor that determines coaching effectiveness. Having the necessary resources alone does not guarantee effective coaching, but the absence of them under any circumstance guarantees failure. The availability of resources (SLACK) greatly impacts on the DESIRE factor. A manager's willingness to undertake specific coaching tasks largely depends on the SLACK that's available.

CONCLUSION

This paper presents "coaching" as more than a process or a series of "management skills." It presents coaching as a three dimensional framework in which Being, Doing and Having are at the core of effective coaching.

"Being" believed (CREDIBILITY) and motivated (DESIRE) are essential factors for any coaching initiative to succeed – together they form the 1st dimension of the coaching model. "Doing" the job (SKILLS) is the 2nd dimension to the model. Finally, "Having" adequate resources (SLACK) is the 3rd dimension of the model.

REFERENCES

Atkinson, C. et al. *Management Development Roles: Coach, Sponsor and Mentor*, Personnel Journal. November, 1980.

Bird, A. *Team Structure and Success as Related to Cohesiveness and Leadership*. Journal of Social Psychology, pp. 103, 217-233, 1977.

Blake, R. & Mouton, J. *The Managerial Grid* (1964). In Hein, H. R., Psychological Type, Coaching Activities and Coaching Effectiveness in Corporate Middle Managers. Dissertation, University of Bridgeport, 1989.

Appendix

Chiaramonte P. & Higgins, A. *Coaching for High Performance*. Business Quarterly, Autumn, pp. 17-23, 1993.

Chelladurai, P. & Saleh, S. D. *Dimensions of Leadership Behavior in Sports: Development of a leadership scale*. Journal of Sport Psychology, pp. 2, 34-45, 1980.

Clark, P. R. & Fry, D. *Coaching Writers-Editors and Reporters Working Together*. New York, St. Martin's Press, 1992.

Cratty, B. J. *Psychology in Contemporary Sport. Guideline for Coaches and Athletes*. Englewoods Cliffs, NJ, Prentice Hall Inc., 1983.

Danielson, R. R., Zelhart, P.F. & Drake, D.J. *Multidimensional Scaling and Factor Analysis of Coaching Behavior as Perceived by High School Hockey Players*. Research Quarterly, pp. 46, 323-334, 1975.

Deegan, A.X. *Coaching: A Management Skill for Improving Individual Performance*. Reading, MA, Addison-Wesley Training Systems, 1979.

Fournies, F. F. *Coaching for Improved Work Performance*. New York, Van Nostrand and Reinhold Company, 1978.

Hein, H. R. *Psychological Type, Coaching Activities and Coaching Effectiveness in Corporate Middle Managers*. Dissertation, University of Bridgeport, 1989.

House, R. J. *A Path – Goal Theory of Leader Effectiveness*. Administrative Science Quarterly, pp. 16, 321-338, 1971.

Kirkpatrick, D. L. *How to Improve Performance Through Appraisal and Coaching*. American Management Association, 1982.

LeUnes, A. D. & Nation, J. R. *Sport Psychology, An Introduction*. Chicago, Nelson-Hall, 1989.

Locke, E. & Latham, G. *The Application of Goal Setting to Sports*. In LeUnes, A. D. & Nation, J. R., Sport Psychology: An Introduction. Chicago, Nelson-Hall, 1989.

Lovin, B. C. & Casstevens, E. R. *Coaching, Learning and Action*. American Management Association, 1971.

Mahler, W. *The Coaching Practices Survey. Diagnostics Studies*. Reading, MA, Addison-Wesley from Hein (1989) pp. 47-55, 1974.

Mahler, W. & Wrightnour, W. F. *Executive Continuity: How to Build and Retain an Effective Management Team*. Honewood, IL, Dow Jones-Irwin Inc., 1973.

Megginson, D. & Boydell, T. *A Manager's Guide to Coaching* (1986). In Hein, H. R., Psychological Type, Coaching Activities and Coaching Effectiveness in Corporate Middle Managers. Dissertation, University of Bridgeport, 1989.

Murray, M. C. & Mann, B. L. *Leadership Effectiveness*. In Williams, J. W., Ed., Applied Sport Psychology, Mayfield Publishing Company, 1993.

Orth, C., Wilkinson, H. & Benfari, R. *The Manager's Role as Coach and Mentor* (1987). In Hein, H. R., Psychological Type, Coaching Activities and Coaching Effectiveness in Corporate Middle Managers. Dissertation, University of Bridgeport, 1989.

Peters, T. J., Austin, N. K. *A Passion for Excellence: The Leadership Difference*. New York, Random House Inc., 1985.

Rochefort, G. R. *A Comparative Analysis of Sport and Business Coaching*. Montreal, Unpublished, 1994.

Sabock, A. *The Coach*. In LeUnes, A.D. & Nation, J. R., Sport Psychology: An Introduction. Chicago, Nelson-Hall, 1979.

Sage, G. H. *Sport and American Society: Selected Readings*, Second Edition. Reading, MA, Addison-Wesley, 1974.

Sinclair, D. A. & Vealy, R. S. *Effects of Coaches' Expectations and Feedback on the Self-Perceptions of Athletes*, Journal of Sport Behaviour, 1989.

Singer, E. J. *Effective Management Coaching*. Institute of Personnel Management. Great Britain, David Green (Printers) Ltd., 1974.

Veissier, J. C. *Le coaching: de la gestion de la performance sportive a la gestion de la performance en entreprise*. H.E.C, novembre, 1993.

Yager, E. *Coaching Models*. Executive Excellence, March 1993.

Index

Index

For more information about our services

contact

PMC-Management Coaching

629 Lyman Boulevard, Newmarket, Ontario, Canada, L3X 1V9

Tel (905) 954-1875, Fax (905) 954-0787

e-mail info@pmcoaching.com

www.pmcoaching.com